Highland and Other Jottings

by Lizzie Kate

To Peter & Betty

Here's to the Memories !

Pauline

6cl/95

Highland and Other Jottings

by Lizzie Kate

Elizabeth C. Sherry

The Pentland Press Limited
Edinburgh • Cambridge • Durham

First published in 1994 by
The Pentland Press Ltd.
1 Hutton Close
South Church
Bishop Auckland
Durham

ISBN 1 85821 238 3

Typeset by CBS, Felixstowe, Suffolk
Printed and bound by Antony Rowe Ltd., Chippenham

Dedicated
to
Joe

With thanks to my own
and my husband's family

Also to my friends for their
encouragement

FOREWORD

My main reason for writing this book, as I mentioned in the Epilogue, was to help me during a very sad period in my life.

I found writing about happier times was of great therapeutic value. We hear so many tales of doom and gloom nowadays, so I thought that recalling some of my funnier mishaps might bring a smile to the reader's face and so brighten his or her day.

Several people have asked me why Lizzie Kate. My Christian names are Elizabeth Cathrine and when we were children my brother called me Lizzie Kate. He encouraged me when I started to write and also confirmed certain details regarding our early family life. Sadly, he did not live to see the book published and so I felt that using his special name in the title would be a sort of tribute to him.

Elizabeth C. Sherry
1994

CHAPTER 1

I had a very happy childhood, brought up in a farming community in the beautiful Highlands of Scotland. I think the countryside is the ideal environment in which to bring up young children.

I recently heard on a TV programme, a certain area in Britain described as being 'in the back of beyond'. I wondered then if the TV presenter would define my birthplace in the same way. I decided to investigate a little and looked up in the dictionary to discover that the back of beyond is a 'remote inaccessible spot'. I must, therefore, come to the conclusion that I was born in the back of beyond because it was almost inaccessible with very infrequent means of transport.

Another phrase frequently used nowadays is 'in the middle of nowhere'. A further search in the dictionary revealed nowhere as 'not in any place or state', so how can nowhere have a middle when it does not exist?

The reader might think the above meandering is not relevant to my story but then, a little divergence, I think, lends a bit of interest.

I often think, like Dr Who, it would be wonderful to go back in time and if I had that ability I would choose the middle of the last century. Everything I know about my ancestors I learned through stories handed down by members of my family. This is one of the reasons why I want to put what I know down in print because life, even when I was a child, was vastly different from what it is today.

My great-grandfather was the blacksmith in the district where my family lived. His smithy, or smiddy, was roughly where the Flying Club hangar now stands at Inverness Airport. When the airport was built just before World War Two, there was a road leading to several cottages, which was called 'the smiddy road' by the local people. In the last century this road ended at the blacksmith's smiddy.

1

There were no tractors, of course, at that time, so horses were used on all the farms. The wealthier people had horses to draw the carriages they used, just as they would use cars today. The blacksmith in any rural community was, therefore, a very busy man and my great-grandfather was no exception.

He had so much work to cope with he had to employ another blacksmith to help him. I wondered how people advertised for staff in the nineteenth century. However, after making a quick telephone call I discovered the *Inverness Courier* began publication one hundred and seventy years ago so *it* might be the answer to my question.

A young man called Thomas MacDonald applied for the job and he was successful - in fact he was successful in more ways than one because he married the boss's daughter. They had twelve children - ten of whom survived to adulthood. My father was the youngest of the family so we had cousins almost as old as my father.

After I went to school and started to enjoy the magic of fairy stories I used to imagine Granny as the beautiful princess who married the handsome prince. Handsome he might have been, but if he was anything like Longfellow's Village Blacksmith he would not have looked like the slim, handsome prince in the story books.

My grandfather died when my father was only six months old. He died suddenly, and it seems he had no previous history of heart trouble. The shock was so great, Granny told me years later, her teeth all fell out. It seems funny now, but it must have been a great blow to her. She never had false teeth in her life and you would think she would look old and decrepit. This was not the case, however, and I have a studio photograph taken when she was in her seventies and, even toothless, she was a beautiful lady. She was ninety when she died and her hair was still a lovely auburn shade with not a single grey strand.

My maternal grandmother died when my mother was only thirteen years old so we, as a family, knew only one grandmother.

Some of my earliest memories are of time spent in the company of my father's mother. She was born in the middle of the last century, just a hundred years after the Battle of Culloden. Her actual date of birth was 18th March 1848. I know this because she told me so often I could not possibly forget. She was nearly eighty when I was born and seemed to remember things that happened a long time ago though she was not

2

so clear about the, then, present time.

Granny and I spent a lot of time together. For years I thought it was because I was her special favourite — or perhaps as I was the middle child in a family of five. The other reason I thought it might be was that I was the only one with two Christian names. This was not due to any favouritism on the part of my parents, they just could not decide which of two aunts I was to be called after. They solved that problem by calling me after both. Now I realize that the reason Granny spent so much time with me was to take some of the burden off my mother's shoulders at the start of my father's last illness.

My father died at the age of thirty-seven, leaving a wife and five children, the youngest, one and a half years old, and the eldest nearly ten. My father had tuberculosis - the scourge of the earlier part of the twentieth century. He was never in hospital but, to keep him apart from the children, he had a little house in the garden with windows all round. My mother, who really was a saint, nursed him and also looked after five children and an elderly mother-in-law.

I discovered a brass bell in a cupboard many years later and asked my mother about it. She told me that during my father's illness the bell hung in the house. It was connected to my father's little house by a cord which my father pulled when he required attention. I often think about my mother's life in those days and wonder how she managed to cope with everything. Cope she certainly did, and throughout her long life she retained a sunny disposition which gained her friends wherever she went.

My two older sisters were in school and I was just four and a half, so even taking one child off her hands must have been a relief for my poor mother. Granny and I had little outings to visit her sister and some of her friends. Her sister, our great-aunt, was a widow and lived in a croft about a mile and a half from our house. It does not seem far but as Granny was eighty-two and I was just over four our legs could not cope with the distance. We therefore took the bus - quite an experience in those days when public transport did not run as frequently as it does today.

It was summer when we had our outings and the days were always long and sunny, or is my memory playing tricks? I remember we used to

3

sit for ages on the bank at the side of the road waiting for the bus to come along. We were all dressed up in our Sunday best and both wore hats - Granny's a fancy black one to match her widow's weeds and mine a light coloured straw with little flowers all round.

Granny and her sister enjoyed each other's company and caught up with family news. As not many people, certainly not among our friends, had telephones, this was about the only way to pass on news, except by letter.

We were able to walk to her friends who lived in a small fishing community not very far from our house. On our way we passed a beautiful oak wood called the *darach*. The name is Gaelic for oak and is only one of the many places in the area known by the Gaelic translation of their names.

Granny told me that in olden times some people would not pass the *darach* at night because it was supposed to be haunted. They said ghosts were seen at the lower end of the wood. In reality, there was an illicit still and, of course, the people making the whisky did not want to be discovered. On moonlit nights they put white sheets over their heads and danced around, so giving rise to the story of the ghosts. Granny did not tell me the story of the ghosts etc., until much later when I was a few years older.

Now, I cannot vouch for the authenticity of this story, but who am I to doubt such a trustworthy person as Granny? There is only one thing that puzzles me - and that is, how was it Granny was so knowledgeable about the dark deeds at the bottom of the wood? I know she was a good dancer in her young days, but was her dancing confined to the dance floor, I ask myself?

There were about a dozen houses in the small community which we visited. Each household owned a small rowing boat and the men went out fishing each day, mainly for herring. The women then set out with the fish in creels on their backs to sell the previous day's catch. Granny told me they even walked as far as Inverness which was about eight miles away.

It was a hard life but it was the only one they knew and fishing was in their blood. There were no fishing restrictions then as there are today. I suppose none were required because fishing, in our area at least, was only what could be caught from a small boat.

4

I read recently that at one time, in a small community like ours, a person was known by a single Christian name. As the population grew it was necessary to develop the name further so as to prevent confusion.

Quite often a surname was derived from a man's occupation. Thus, in the case of our family, we could have had the surname Smith because our grandfather was a blacksmith. However, as his ancestors were the sons of Donald our surname became MacDonald.

The majority of people in the Highland fishing villages had, and still have, the same surname although all the families are not related. They are not usually the Macs of the Scottish clan system but quite often are a derivation of a Scandinavian name.

A great deal of confusion could be caused because of many families having the same name - so nicknames were used and have passed down through generations. The strange thing is, the sons were given as surname their mother's Christian name, for example, John Annie or James Rachel or William Maggie. It may seem peculiar to outsiders but to the people of the village it was a simple way to distinguish between the sons of families when describing a certain incident. How the postman knew where to deliver mail is a mystery to me! The problem has now been solved for the postman as the houses have been given names.

Granny's friends were the older members of the families whose working days were over. I sometimes wonder if I was something of a hindrance to the cosy chats which were enjoyed by the friends. They sometimes spoke in Gaelic which was their native tongue. I think now, it may have been because the subject under discussion was not suitable for a child's ears. I was speaking recently to an elderly lady who came from the Western Isles. She told me her parents used the same system when she was a child, but the other way round. When her parents wanted to talk privately they spoke in English to each other as the children only knew Gaelic.

During our visits Granny and her friends took snuff while they chatted to each other. This may seem an unusual thing for women to do, and also a dirty habit, but not any more so, I think, than smoking today. While all this was going on I sat happily eating bread and jam. I was no child genius and yet I vividly remember all our outings. I wonder if it is because I enjoyed them so much. I certainly do not remember any unhappiness in those days, and yet my mother must have had a very hard life though she always seemed calm and never bad-tempered.

I mentioned earlier about my two Christian names. I have just remembered another difference of opinion at the time of my birth. Granny, as head of the family, I suppose, laid down the law at times. One stipulation she made was that the first son of each member of her family was to be called Thomas after her husband and our grandfather.

I was the third daughter to arrive in our branch so, thinking a son might not put in an appearance, Granny said, 'You can call her Thomasina and then shorten it to Sina.' My mother, not usually a quarrelsome sort of person, took the unusual step of rebelling and said, 'supposing I have a dozen daughters not one of them will be called Thomasina.' Mother told me this many years later and I thanked her for my lucky escape from Sina.

I have never been able to understand why parents have their child christened one name and then shorten it to a different one. I should have thought it would be much easier to call the child by the abbreviated name right from the start.

I started school a few months before my father died. The teacher had also taught my father so she must have been quite old. Perhaps teachers carried on working until they were no longer fit to do so rather than be forced to retire at a certain age as happens nowadays.

When I started school the teacher cycled to work, as she had done in my father's day, and her home was about four miles away. Some years later she bought a small car which must have made life a lot easier for her after struggling along in all weathers on the bicycle.

My aunt told me that for their annual outing the pupils assembled at the school and brought their own food. The teacher had her bicycle and said to the children, 'I'll mount and you run after.' They then set off walking or running to the appointed place to have games and their picnic. I wonder how they ever managed to have enough energy to play games after following a bicycle for a couple of miles. So much for 'the good old days'!

During our schooldays the outings were usually to the seashore of the Inner Moray Firth. I suppose the teachers considered it quite a suitable location as it was within walking distance of the school and also had plenty of space for games. It wasn't really a novelty for our family as we spent most days in summer on the beach anyway.

I find it quite funny that the edge of the sea is known by different names in various parts of Britain. We always called it the shore or the beach. The older people called it by the Gaelic name the *traigh*, pronounced 'try', or the *clattach* which, translated, means a stony beach. I have heard people in the south-west of Scotland refer to it as the coast when they say, for instance, 'we'll go for a run to the coast.' In England, on the other hand, it is called the seaside or the beach.

We were only a ten minute walk from the beach and we spent many happy hours there during our summer holidays. Even today, people who do not know the Highlands have the mistaken idea that we still live in the Ice Age and that both summer and winter are bitterly cold. I think ours would be called a temperate climate. During our childhood the summer days were usually warm and sunny with the occasional thunder-storm which helped to ease the, sometimes, heavy sultry conditions.

My mother used to pack food for our days on the beach and we set off, each one carrying a small container with provisions for our picnic. My mother must have looked like a mother duck with all the little ducklings following behind, for as many of our small friends who wished to would join us.

The beach was pebbly but when the tide was out there were huge stretches of firm wet sand on which to play and also rock pools to explore. There were large mussel beds which we had to avoid as they were too sharp for small feet to walk over. The local fishermen used to gather the mussels as bait. Nowadays these are part of the menu in expensive restaurants. It really is amazing how times have changed!

As we sat having our picnic lunch and gazing across the firth we used to see creatures that we called porpoises leaping along in the water. Recently, the Moray Firth dolphins have had a great deal of press coverage. I read an article in one of the local newspapers which explained the difference between dolphins and porpoises. It seems that dolphins leap out of the water and porpoises cruise along on the surface, so probably we watched the ancestors of the present dolphins.

Mother told us not to wander along the beach in an easterly direction as that part belonged to the farmer who was our neighbours and who went swimming there. It was not until many years later that I discovered the real reason for the ban. I knew the seashore was common ground and not owned by anyone. I asked my mother why we were not supposed to go in a certain direction when we were children. She told me our neighbour went swimming in his birthday suit so she felt it unwise to allow five pairs of young eyes to watch the proceedings. She must have made the mistake of wandering along that way herself and discovered the 'bare facts'.

There was something else about the beach which I did not know about until much later. I always thought that when the tide went out on our side of the firth it must have gone in on the other side. This is not the case, of course, as both tides go out and in simultaneously.

I understand the tides are affected by the phases of the moon. The high, or spring, tide every four weeks coincides with the full moon. Again we have a high tide with the new moon. Tides between those high tides are referred to as neap tides. Another foray in the dictionary disclosed further facts about this interesting subject:

High Tide or Spring Tide: Maximum tide when the sun's attraction is pulling in conjunction with the moon's.

Neap Tide: Minimum tide when sun's attraction is pulling contrary to the moon's.

(I regret repetition of the word 'tide'.)

There was another reason for our visits to the seashore throughout the summer and autumn. My mother made all the jam we used so a great deal of fruit was required. We had a large garden and grew lots of soft fruit bushes and also fruit trees. However, as wild raspberries grew in abundance, and the jam made from them is far superior to that from garden fruit, we spent many hours picking our own. The raspberries were easy to pick as the bushes were quite low with the fruit easily accessible.

The brambles, later on in the season, were quite a different matter. The raspberries were ripe in July when the days were long, warm and sunny. Bramble gathering could not be done until the fruit ripened in October when winter was fast approaching and little hands were cold as they did the picking.

We used to wonder why the biggest, most luscious berries were always at the top of the highest bushes and were quite unreachable.

Many hands really do make light work, though, and with a mother and five children working hard the baskets were soon filled.

There is something very gratifying about seeing a pan of jam bubbling away on the cooker in a warm, cosy kitchen after a day spent in the cold gathering the fruit.

CHAPTER 2

There were no school meals in the thirties so we all took our own food and the teachers dished out hot water for our cocoa. Some children had oatcakes and cheese but most, like we did, took bread and jam. I used to think 'I wish we could have bought jam like some of the other children.' I realize now that home-made was much better and certainly cheaper when fruit was there for the picking. It is just another case of the grass being greener on the other side of the fence.

Modern farming is entirely different from what it was when we were children. Horses were still used in the rural community where we lived. Fields were quite small, with the hedges or stone dykes dividing them providing nesting sites for birds. Wildlife was more abundant as there were no pesticides used which have, since then, killed off so many small animals and birds. Rabbits and hares were also plentiful as this was a long time before myxomatosis was introduced with such cruel results.

The crops grown were oats and barley, also turnips and potatoes. The whisky trade was much more prosperous then than it is today so the demand for barley was great. Oats were more widely used as more people ate porridge and oatcakes. The usual measure bought for family use was a boll of oatmeal. I understand it was one hundred and forty pounds but this measure is no longer used.

Horses pulled the machinery which was used to cultivate the land. I was talking to a man recently who worked on the farm when he was a teenager in the thirties. He remembered with much affection the horses which were used on the farm. They were always harnessed in pairs to pull the machinery, so he spoke about them in that way. Their names were Punch and Tibby, Clyde and Maran, Dick and Star, Jock and Beaut, and Nell and Betty.

They were heavy Clydesdale horses and I have often wondered why

11

certain names were chosen for them. We always thought of the horses as our friends and I cannot imagine the present day tractor being thought of in the same affectionate way. This does not mean that I am biased in favour of the 'good old days'. I was only a very young onlooker then and it was not until much later I realized the real hardship which the farmworkers endured.

Although it was hard work, with long hours, the farmworkers seemed quite contented with their way of life. I understand they started work at 5.30a.m. in spring and summer with shorter working hours in winter as work could only be done in daylight. The first job in the morning was to clean out the stables and then feed the horses before going to the fields.

I still think one of the loveliest sights of the countryside was a horse-drawn plough turning over the furrow, with flocks of seagulls flying behind collecting worms which had been turned up by the plough.

I think our favourite time as children was when we saw the binder arriving in the harvest field to start cutting the grain. We didn't help with the harvest but were just interested spectators. The binder cut the crop and then threw out the sheaves of corn or barley. There were extra helpers employed at that time to stook the sheaves so that the sun and wind would dry the grain.

The harvest was then taken to the farmyard where, eventually, the threshing mill would arrive to finish the job. Mill day was a busy time for everyone and for none more so than the farmer's wife who supplied cooked lunches for all the workers.

The mill man was self-employed and spent his time travelling round all the farms in the district. The farmers had to book the mill in advance and the casual workers were employed by each farmer in turn. Nowadays the combine harvester completes the job which was originally done by the binder and threshing mill.

In the long bright evenings we used to play hide-and-seek among the stooks in the harvest field. We did no harm to the crop and it was an ideal place for our game. Our neighbouring farmer was very easy going (or easy oasy to use the local description) so he didn't mind our playing in the fields. I think children brought up in a rural area learn, at an early age, to respect the countryside and all the birds and animals that live there.

My youngest sister and I were friendly with two girls whose fathers worked on the farm. You might say we were the original 'Gang of Four', to use a fairly recent political expression. As oldest member and leader, like Just William, I organized games and usually all went well. However, I became too ambitious, or perhaps, as so often happens with leaders, the sense of power went to my head. I held meetings to arrange certain outings, usually to the seashore or to explore the local wood or *darach* which was mentioned in an earlier chapter. The outing I am about to describe was to be the last for some time.

I don't think I was domineering, more the slave driver with velvet gloves, and the members of the gang really were my willing slaves. If I had said, 'we'll climb Ben Wyvis' they would have agreed to it. That is the kind of loyalty I was given.

The local village was about three miles away and I decided we would go there on the Friday evening after school. I was mature enough to realize that we would be quite tired the following morning – hence the reason for choosing Friday. We pooled our resources and discovered we had one shilling and sixpence among the four of us. That was seven and a half pence in today's money which may not seem much but in the thirties it was a fortune to some youngsters.

The main reason for the shortage of funds was that weekly pocket money was an unheard of thing to us. Our two friends had older sisters and brothers who were working and gave them the odd penny. My sister and I often had visiting relatives who sometimes slipped us the small coin from time to time.

The chief purpose of the expedition was to visit a general store in the village which had the most wonderful selection of sweets. A small bar of chocolate could be bought for a penny so all the way to the village we talked about how we would spend our fortune.

We didn't mention to anybody where we were going because it was a secret and little girls love secrets. We never understood afterwards why the grown-ups made such a fuss. We had a lovely walk to the village but it took longer than usual because we stopped to examine various flowers by the roadside and also looked in bushes for birds' nests.

We were very excited about the visit to the shop and even if we had had five pounds it would not have needed more planning. When we did eventually reach the shop we stood for ages looking at the vast selection of sweets before making our purchases.

We then started on the long trek back but, for some reason, the road was twice as long as it had been on the outward journey. I was the eldest at eleven years old and the youngest was only seven and small legs got tired easily. It was also starting to get dark and, to tired young people, small animals scurrying by the side of the road seemed like lions or tigers.

We were away about four hours altogether and the families were frantic with worry, not knowing what could have happened to us. They must have thought it was a Scottish case of the Pied Piper who had enticed the children away. By the time we reached home, absolutely exhausted, the thrill of the secret expedition and all the sweets had lost their appeal. We had eaten most of the sweets, anyway, and were feeling decidedly queasy.

Worse was to come because the mothers, instead of the hugs and sympathy we expected, had decided punishment was the only answer. I expect after the worry they endured, the relief, instead of bringing tears of joy, had made them angry. They must have had a council of war because we were all meted out the same treatment which was no supper and hot bottoms all round. We weren't too bothered about the lack of food as we had eaten far too many sweets but the spanking, I think, hurt our pride more than our skins.

As I said at the beginning of this sad tale, there were no outings allowed for quite some time. It was to be games near at home until we could be trusted once more. I must say this about my fellow culprits, they never showed any resentment towards me for organizing such a fiasco. My eldest sister met a lady recently whose own sister was one of the gang and said they still talk about the night of the missing children.

We were partly self-supporting in the food line, which meant we were a little better off than a family living in a city in the same financial position. We grew our own fruit and vegetables and also kept poultry.

In the spring, when a hen went broody, my mother set thirteen eggs under her (why thirteen and not twelve, I wonder?) Before the hen was set my mother did a little experiment which I shall now describe. I do not know if this is a Highland custom for I have never heard or read about it being done by anyone else.

My mother took off her wedding ring and slipped a length of silk thread through it. She then held the ring over each egg in turn. If the ring went in a circle the chicken which would eventually emerge from the egg would be a pullet, whereas if it swung to and fro a cockerel would hatch. The reason for this test was because my mother wanted as many pullets as possible to provide eggs. I do not know if it was always accurate but it was done each time a hen was set.

A cosy nest was made for the hen in a coop, or little house, and after a few weeks the gorgeous baby chicks hatched. They were like the fluffy chickens seen on Easter eggs or cakes and spent their time scratching around in their little run with mother hen fussing over them. We were all very excited when the first chicks arrived and took it in turn to feed them.

Our other source of food came from a dozen beehives which were situated at the far end of the garden. My father had started bee-keeping and after he died my mother decided to continue with it. It provided some extra financial help and also a nutritious food for the family. My mother's brother lived near us and he offered to do most of the work in tending the bees. He loved doing it and I can understand why, as it is such a fascinating occupation.

My mother explained to us the intricate process of honey production so we were the more interested when we helped to prepare for it in the spring. Comb honey bought in shops is made by the bees in small wood sections. Nowadays, most honey is sold in jars and the only comb honey seems to be found in health shops. When we were young there were quite a number of bee-keepers in the district and all sold comb honey. As twelve hives needed a vast number of sections we all helped by fitting the wax foundation into the wooden sections. The best honey came from clover nectar in summer, and heather in autumn.

There does not seem to be much clover in fields or at the roadside nowadays so I wonder from where the bulk of the honey comes. There certainly does not appear to be the same quantity of Scottish honey sold in shops but the reason may be that the foreign honey is so much cheaper that the traders are able to sell more. If this is the case I find it quite sad as I think Scottish honey must be the finest in the world.

In my mother's bee-keeping days there were plenty fields of clover within easy reach of our hives and the wood beside the house had an abundant supply of heather. Some of the bee-keepers were not so lucky and did not have vast stretches of heather growing near their house. Many of them transported their hives to the nearest heather moor and brought them back in late autumn when the season was over.

The greatest worry for bee-keepers in summer is swarming, especially on hot sultry days when bees are most inclined to leave the hive as a swarm. It was always a disaster to lose a swarm, especially when only a small number of hives were kept. The bees never seemed to fly too far away from the hive so it was usually quite simple to locate the swarm. Although swarms happened mostly on hot days the weather was not the reason for its happening.

It is the old queen bee who leads the swarm, but not before the younger queens are ready to take over her duties in the hive. When the swarm had settled, usually in a tree, my mother then set off with a skep (a straw beehive) and white tablecloth to collect it. White seemed to attract the bees so the cloth was thrown over them in their cluster. They were then transferred to the skep and my mother got someone to help her to carry them home. Afterwards my uncle arrived to finish the operation by getting them into an empty hive.

My explanation of the intricacies of bee-keeping may not be too detailed but I have done my best to show why we, as children, found it so fascinating.

There were several vans which delivered groceries, butcher meat and bread to the rural areas. My mother bought meat and bread from the vans but our groceries were delivered by Dai who had a shop in the village. His name was David but everyone called him Dai - it would seem a name heard more in the Welsh valleys than in the Highlands of Scotland. He had a horse and cart and must have taken hours to pack all the groceries into it. The farm carts were deep but Dai's was shallow and held a huge amount of groceries, including bags of oatmeal. As the cart was open on top it was covered with a large waterproof sheet, or tarpaulin to give it the proper name.

Dai was a dapper little man and was well clad, especially in the winter. He had a seat up on the cart with no protection against the elements so waterproof clothing really was a necessity.

Winters were really severe compared with those of today. I understand the reason given by the experts for the climatic change is something called 'global warming'. As I am not an expert I can only accept their word and quote from what I have heard.

Roads were often closed because they were blocked by drifting snow. Ben Wyvis, which is just across the firth from where we lived, was often mentioned when the weather was being discussed. Someone would say, 'we'll get snow before evening – the ben has a white cap', or, 'we're bound to get snow – that wind is coming straight off the ben.'

The weather pattern has changed completely now and many parts of England get far more frost and snow than we do. Our local newspaper gives daily weather temperatures in Britain and throughout the world. I have kept many of the cuttings since December 1991 just in case anyone may query the authenticity of the above statement.

I have strayed slightly from the story of Dai and I shall now pick it up where I left off. The men who were employed by the county roads department did a good job clearing the snow so Dai managed to do his rounds in all weathers.

He visited our area on Tuesdays and Fridays and was on the road from early morning until late evening. Dai's day was long because he did not rush from house to house but took time to sell his merchandise and also to talk to his customers about their daily lives and families. Some of the people shared their meals with him and he had lots of cups of tea throughout the day. If any of his customers suddenly discovered they had run out of a certain commodity from the food cupboard all they had to do was wait for Dai at the side of the road and he would gladly serve them. This was just as well as there was no supermarket round the corner. I think the personal touch made all the difference. Dai may not have made a fortune but he was liked and respected by all who knew him.

My mother did a sort of barter system at times and paid for the groceries with sections of honey in season. She also sold him eggs and the occasional chicken for his own family. The days of the battery hen had not yet arrived so all hens and chickens were free range. They spent their days scratching around happily with the odd visit to the cosy nests in the henhouse to lay their eggs. There were not so many rules and regulations in those days so people like Dai were able to buy the odd

17

chicken or dozen eggs without restrictions.

Dai was a licensed grocer so I expect some of the people who stopped him by the roadside wanted to buy the odd bottle of *uisge beatha,* or water of life to use the English translation. The days of getting supplies from the illicit still in the *darach* were long gone.

It was said Dai drank some of the profits himself to keep the cold out on the winter nights and who could blame him? I understand the horse made its own way home with Dai sitting up on his seat in the cart, half asleep but I'm sure with a happy smile on his face. I still remember, quite clearly, the sound of the horse clip clopping along the road on a frosty night. Although we did not live by the side of the road the sound carried on a clear night.

CHAPTER 3

My mother encouraged us to take an interest in the flora and fauna of the countryside around us. One source of interest was some clayholes in the wood on the other side of our garden fence. The clay had been dug out and used as mortar in the building trade. This practice had long since ceased so the holes, because of the clay foundation, retained rain water.

There was an abundance of wildfowl, especially moorhen and woodcock. The clayholes were teeming with frogs and toads whose tadpoles in spring formed part of the moorhens' diet. Many survived, of course, and reached maturity as the paddocks (Scottish name for frogs) were to be seen on many of the adjacent woodland paths.

As the trees grew, their roots sucked up the water in the clayholes so the frogs, toads and wildfowl all disappeared. I wonder if this has happened throughout Britain now that frogs and toads are so scarce today. I do not mean that there are clayholes all over the country, but the pools of water necessary for frogs to spawn must have disappeared.

The wood beside our house was a young fir plantation and beyond that was the *darach*, one of our favourite childhood haunts. Here was the home of the red squirrel because, as well as oak, there were also beech trees. In late autumn we used to see the odd squirrel collecting beechmast for his winter larder.

Tawny owls also were resident in the *darach* but were rarely seen as they are nocturnal birds. We used to hear them, especially on moonlit nights. I do not know the reason why they were heard more often on bright nights as they must have been able to see in the dark anyway. It may have been that their prey, which was mainly mice and small birds, came out more often when the moon was brightest.

There were masses of toadstools under the trees in the *darach*. Many years later I used to take my three year old niece there for a walk. One day she asked me why the toadstools were in rings so I told her the story about the wood-pixies coming out at night and, when having a picnic, they used the toadstools as seats.

The following week, when we went for our walk she whispered to me, 'will they still be here?' I told her the pixies lived in the wood and she believed me just as I had never doubted Granny's word nearly thirty years before.

Another story I told was about a little girl called Katy taking her dog for a walk to the *darach*. It was a frosty morning and the spiders' webs on the lower branches of the fir trees were frozen and looked like silver. Katy heard a small voice calling for help and looking up she saw a tiny wood-pixie caught by his wing in the frozen web. Katy was just tall enough to be able to breathe on the web and release the wing. She then carried the little pixie along the path in the fir wood and on to his home in the bank at the far end of the *darach*.

I now tell similar stories to my niece's children and it gives me just as much pleasure as it did over twenty years ago. Fairy stories are always popular with young children, I think, as they transport them into a world where all things are possible. I sometimes think I have retained a part of my childhood mind. This may be why the young hairdresser said to me recently, 'you don't look old,' with the emphasis on the word 'look'. I think what she really meant was, 'I know you are old but you don't *look* it.'

My eldest sister gained a bursary to Inverness Academy and we all felt very proud of her. The other members of the family followed in her footsteps but she was the first.

The bus timetable was not suitable so she travelled to and from Inverness by train. The train was affectionately known by all the rail travellers as 'The Puggy'. I do not know how the name originated but it gave its passengers a happy, friendly way to commute to school or work.

In order to reach the railway station from our house we had to walk through the wood previously mentioned, and then along a road which ended at the station.

My sister wasn't the bravest person in the dark but managed the morning walk all right. However, she was not too happy about the dark winter evenings so my mother, resourceful as ever, decided to take a lantern and meet the nervous traveller. I do not know if torches were available at that time but we certainly did not own one. I think our lamp was called a storm lantern and was fuelled by paraffin. It had quite a powerful light so I expect to my sister, stepping into the darkness from the brightly lit train, it must have been as comforting as a lighthouse is to a sailor making his way home in a stormy sea.

Once the lamp was lit my mother set off to meet my sister. My older sister went with her while Granny looked after the younger children. On the other hand, it may have been a case of the younger children looking after Granny as she was nearly ninety by then.

I sometimes think my mother's nightly journey with the lamp must have been rather like Wordsworth's poem 'Lucy Gray' only with the roles reversed. Instead of Lucy setting off with the lantern in search of her mother my own mother went to meet my sister, alias Lucy Gray. By the time my next sister was ready to attend the academy there was a suitable bus service so it was not necessary to continue with the Lucy Gray routine.

Not having a radio or television to entertain us during the long winter evenings, we were encouraged to read from the collection of children's classics which mother had acquired over the years. As many of our cousins were so much older than us their books were often handed down to us. The books had such an impact I can still remember the stories clearly.

My favourite character from Beatrix Potter was Peter Rabbit and I used to worry terribly about his escapades and hoped he would not be put in a pie by Mrs MacGregor as had happened to his father. I can still see his little blue waistcoat caught in the wire-netting as he made his escape from Mr MacGregor's garden.

Hans Andersen and Grimm's fairy tales were also much loved. Some of the more advanced books I enjoyed were *Little Women, Good Wives*, the Katy books and later still *Wuthering Heights, Jane Eyre, David Copperfield* and *Oliver Twist*. Like most children, to us the characters in the stories were not fictional but real people and we felt sorry for them or shared their happiness, depending on the story line.

Old Angus was one of the more colourful characters of my childhood. Today he would have the grand title 'Vermin Extermination Officer' but in the thirties he was merely called 'Angus the Ratcatcher'. He travelled round the farms and did his best to get rid of the farmer's most hated enemy, the rat.

In those days, in the farming communities, TV and even radio were almost unheard of so people entertained themselves in their leisure time. There were cottages for farmworkers who were married and had families. The single men lived in bothies and managed to cope with the most basic cooking and domestic chores. Their possessions consisted of the bare essentials and they were quite happy to have a table, some chairs and a bed. They did their cooking on an open fire and their meal usually consisted of soup made with a piece of boiling beef and vegetables, with boiled potatoes taken with the beef. It certainly was not a varied diet but was quite wholesome.

On Saturday nights the local men met in one of the bothies. Married men were glad to have a night away from their wives and children and have a chat or 'blether' as it was called with their fellow farmworkers. I expect they became more talkative as the evening wore on with the help of a wee drop of 'the craitur'.

The Gaelic name for their meetings was a *ceilidh* and all were welcome, especially those who could entertain by singing, telling stories or playing the fiddle.

Old Angus was especially popular as his stories were more far-fetched and, therefore, more interesting than any of the others. He was the Aesop or the Grimm or Hans Andersen of the Highlands. He told stories so often to rapt audiences that it was said he actually believed them himself.

Here is an example of the 'Old Angus Tales' as told by himself. The nets he mentions were for catching fish. 'I was laying out my nets on the shore when a flock of geese landed and got tangled in the nets. I shouted 'Whoosh' to scare them off and they all rose, still caught in the net and me hanging on for grim death. Well, they flew right across the firth and landed in the Black Isle. I thought, how am I going to get home? So I shouted 'Whoosh' again and, would you believe it, they took off again and came back across the firth to land in exactly the same spot. Wasn't that amazing?' Of course, everyone thought it was more than amazing, it was unbelievable. He told the story so often and his audience found it so entertaining they would never question its authenticity.

Another of his tales was about the day he caught ninety-nine rats. One member of his audience had the temerity to ask him why he didn't make it one hundred. Angus retorted, 'do you think I would make myself a liar for one rat?'

Yet another story was about twelve crows, each one standing on a post of the fence surrounding a field. As crows were also the farmer's enemies Angus felt it his duty to deal with them. By sheer good luck he had his gun with him so he took aim and one bullet killed all the crows at one go. I feel they must have been *kamikaze* crows when they stood waiting to be killed as they seemed to do.

Of course, when Angus told the stories they were much more detailed than my abbreviated versions. Like folk tales, they have been handed down through the decades and I heard them from people who had listened to the great 'spinner of yarns' himself.

I have mentioned summer when we were children and the daylight hours which were long with very few hours of darkness. It is still the same, of course, and first time visitors to the north of Scotland are amazed at this land of the midnight sun, although the daylight hours are much longer further north.

We were just as happy in winter and were especially excited when the first snow fell. Our sledges were home-made affairs, knocked together by caring adults out of any materials available. However, they did the job just the same as those bought in shops which, perhaps, were sleeker and looked better.

The road near our house has a slope and is now very busy with airport traffic. In the thirties there were very few cars or vans so that part of the road was ideal for tobogganing and we spent many hours doing just that.

There was also a large pond which in winter was covered in ice so it, too, was a happy playground. When the airport was built the pond was drained and, eventually, accommodation huts were built for members of the R.A.F. who were stationed there.

As the decade of the thirties was drawing to a close so, too, was Granny's long life. On reflection, I realize she had more than a fair share of worry in her life. Three of her sons had become regular soldiers, all of them in the Scots Guards. During the First World War one of them was killed, another taken prisoner, and a third so badly wounded in the leg it gave him trouble for the rest of his life.

Another son went to Australia and after a few years nothing more was heard of him. It was thought he had got a job on a remote sheep farm and must have died there. Her youngest child, our father, also died young, as did two of his sisters.

Towards the end of her life Granny was not able to walk very far. I think one of her last outings was on the coronation day of King George V in May 1937. There was a school sports day and one of the teachers very kindly called to take Granny to the sports ground to watch the proceedings. We were very excited about her sitting there watching us taking part in the games and she thoroughly enjoyed her day out.

The following year she caught her foot in the loose cover of her favourite armchair, fell and broke her hip. I expect the reason she was not taken to hospital would have been because she was too old for the bone to set. She died at home shortly afterwards. It was a time of great sadness for us all.

In the early thirties a very exciting thing happened in our neighbourhood. One day a light aircraft landed in a field not very far from our house. Granny said, 'run along and see the aeroplane - you may never see another one so close.' Little did she know that in a few years time, in fact a year after she died, the same field where the aircraft landed would be part of an R.A.F. station and later still would become Inverness Airport.

The pilot of the plane was none other than Captain Fresson, the pioneer of Highland Airways. We stood there, looking in amazement at the plane and pilot in much the same way as present day children would watch the arrival of astronauts returning from the moon. If anyone had said at the time that a man would walk on the moon the statement would have been received in much the same way as Old Angus's tales, with complete disbelief.

Several of our young friends joined us for the inspection of the plane. Captain Fresson must have thought he had landed in Lilliput when he saw the crowd of small people in the field.

Until quite recently all I knew about Captain Fresson was that he was the pioneer of Highland Airways. He started the air service to the Scottish islands and eventually left for Kenya.

However, with the help of a young librarian in Inverness library, I was able to piece together some details of his very interesting life. His own memoirs, *A Road to the Isles*, is now out of print but I was able to see a copy held by the library.

He was born in 1891 and, because of his interest in flying, joined the R.F.C. in 1914. After being demobbed he ran a private flying service, giving joy rides and aerobatic displays in both Scotland and England.

Eric Linklater, in the foreword to *A Road to the Isles* made two profound comments:

(1) He began his service with a minimum of capital but a maximum of vision.

(2) He was a benefactor as well as pioneer and he created not only Highland Airways but a legend that will endure.

The original airfield was on the outskirts of Inverness, on what is now Longman Industrial Estate. The airfield was officially opened on 17th June 1933 by the Duke and Duchess of Sutherland.

Captain Fresson was the first official carrier of air mail in Britain. He flew in all weathers with no radio facilities, and for twelve months prior to receiving the Royal Air Mail Pennant he had to show outstanding regularity in the mail service.

Between 1930 and 1947 he consolidated the Highlands and Islands Air Services. Orkney Air Service was inaugurated in 1934 and Shetland Air Service in 1936. Captain Fresson maintained them even during the Second World War, with unarmed aircraft and enforced radio silence.

In 1947 British European Airways took over the service, dispersed Captain Fresson's fleet and dismissed him. What a sad ending to such a wonderful career in the Highlands!

The Highland people, however, never forgot him or lost their admiration for him. In 1991, on the centenary of his birth, a statue of him was unveiled at Inverness Airport. There he stands, near where he first landed sixty years before.

The new Inverness Airport was built just before the Second World

War and throughout the war it was an R.A.F. air gunnery school. Our lovely peaceful countryside changed completely, but somehow we seemed to adjust to the new way of life. The same thing happened all over Britain, of course, when airfields sprang up all over the country where, previously, farms had been.

Our school holidays in summer 1939 were extended by a week so that evacuees from Edinburgh could be found temporary homes in the community. Most of the children adapted to the completely new lifestyle very well. It really was amazing that they did because some of them had never seen fields or farm animals in their lives.

I remember one incident regarding the newcomers. The church bell was to the silent for the duration of the war but, in the event of an air raid, it was to be rung. Luckily there were no air raids so far north but one day, on his way home from school, one of the evacuees rang the bell.

There was a rope which was attached to the bell and it hung down the side of the church. The rope was then pulled to enable the bell to be rung. The boy must have jumped up and caught the rope and gave everyone quite a scare. Perhaps he was homesick and just wanted a little excitement in his young life.

When the word went round that the church bell was not to be rung except in the event of an air raid the local people were quite sure it would be silent during the war years. We were a long way from central and south England where most of the air raids happened. It was all the more surprising, therefore, when the peal of bells rang out across the district.

Although the aerodrome, now Inverness Airport, was not an operational station, there was still night flying. I expect it was part of the training for young airmen who, eventually, would have to fly at night while taking part in bombing raids over Germany.

The strange thing was, the members of my family all slept better when the planes were flying at night. It may have been that we felt safer, as though we were being protected by the aeroplanes flying overhead. I find it quite strange even writing about that time in my life. It is as if it was a nightmare which keeps recurring to remind us of all that happened between 1939 and 1945.

There were over forty airmen from the R.A.F. station killed in flying accidents and there is a permanent reminder of this in our local church to this day. Their names were inscribed on wooden plaques which were hung in the station chapel during the war. Afterwards they were removed to the local church.

Although we were a long way from the fighting there were many local young men killed on active service. I remember particularly, a neighbour's daughter coming to our house with the news that the dreaded telegram had arrived. It was to inform the family that the girl's brother had been killed while serving in the navy on Mediterranean patrol.

Our own cousin, also in the navy, was killed while on a convoy to Russia. He had written to his mother, our aunt, to suggest when the film *The Cruel Sea* came to Inverness, she should try to see it. When it did come she asked my mother and brother to accompany her. When they returned to her home after seeing the film the telegram was waiting for her. I don't think she ever really got over that blow.

Our little hamlet consisted of six cottages and out of those, two families were in mourning because of the tragedies I have just described. The phrase 'They also serve who only stand and wait', much quoted at that time, was just as appropriate then as when John Milton wrote it three hundred years before.

There were two occasions during the war when I was responsible for causing my mother a great deal of worry. The first happened in 1940 when I became very ill with peritonitis - something which, even today with modern medical treatment, can be a very serious illness. My mother stayed with an aunt in Inverness and spent most of her day at the hospital.

She told me years later that she was told I was not expected to live more than a week. She found our church minister very supportive at that time and all her life firmly believed in the power of prayer. I think that is what helped her through so many dark periods in her life. The minister said to me years later, 'I remember Matron saying to me, "poor little thing - she hasn't got long to go," and here you are, still hale and hearty.'

I was in the Inverness Royal Infirmary from March until June and

27

was in bed all that time, having had two operations. It is vastly different today when patients in surgical wards are out of bed within days of having their operations.

When my time for leaving the hospital was approaching I used to hear some of the patients asking the nurses, 'any word of the 51st?' It was the time of Dunkirk and the 51st Highland Division suffered such a horrendous number of casualties. Some were taken prisoner but many were killed.

There was another young girl besides myself in the ward – I think probably because we were both gravely ill or perhaps were too old for the children's ward. All the other patients were women and possibly many had husbands or brothers serving with the 51st. It was truly a very dreadful time for the Highland people.

The second time I gave my mother cause for concern was three years later. I had started work in a sub post office and, on my way home one night, fell over a bicycle in the blackout. The bicycle had been carelessly left lying on the pavement when I went for the bus. People who did not live through the war years could never understand how really pitch black towns and cities were in the blackout.

At first I thought I had merely bruised my knee in the accident and the other members of the family used to laugh when I limped around, thinking I was pretending to be lame. It was only when I became delirious it was realized I was quite ill and the doctor diagnosed rheumatic fever. Most patients with this illness were treated in hospital but my mother, true to her caring style, nursed me at home with her usual skill and dedication.

My eldest sister had just got married to one of the airmen from the R.A.F. station. He had brought overseas airmen to the house and they were happy to have a home from home in which to spend some of their off duty time. I was ill for six months but, when I was at the recuperative stage, the Canadian airmen used to bring me what they called candy. This was something which was much appreciated as our sweets were rationed and we had to use our coupons carefully.

When the war ended there were welcome home parties for the service men and women. There was also great sadness for the families whose sons were never coming home.

Midway through the war my eldest sister moved to her new home in south Yorkshire and, both during the war and after, I paid many enjoyable visits to that part of the country. It was a long train journey with two changes - one at Edinburgh and the other at York. I still travel by train whenever possible but feel quite nostalgic for the old steam trains which, although slower and dirtier, had more character than the smooth, sleek modern trains.

I made one of those journeys in 1953 at the time of the coronation. My sister and her husband had a television set - something not every household had at that time. It was a black and white set and the screen was tiny and in a cabinet, not at all like the modern slim-line sets.

To the viewers at that time, however, it was the most marvellous thing to actually see the wonderful events in London on that most historic day. My sister and her husband had invited quite a number of friends to their house for the day and she had prepared a buffet lunch. There were also odd cups of tea and coffee served throughout the day.

At the actual moment the Queen was crowned we all had a drink, stood up, and toasted Her Majesty. The same sort of thing was happening all over the country when her subjects celebrated the coronation of their new monarch. Thousands stood in the pouring rain in London just to get a glimpse of the Queen as her coach made its way to and from Westminster Abbey.

CHAPTER 4

In 1958 I decided I'd like to go on holiday to Norway. People did not go abroad so often at that time so there were not so many tours available. I was very disappointed to be told that the tour I had hoped to do was fully booked. Some time afterwards the travel agents let me know there was a cancellation and asked if I still wanted to have the holiday.

In the meantime the tragic air crash happened at Munich which claimed the lives of so many of the Manchester United football players. I think my mother believed that lightning really can strike twice because she said, 'I don't think you should fly to Norway. I've just heard about a lovely coach tour in Europe which seems much better.'

I decided to take her advice and afterwards was very pleased that I did as I thoroughly enjoyed the tour which was very well organized. As I was the first of our family to travel abroad I wrote about my holiday in a small notebook which was then passed to each member to read. I still have the little book and can now recount some of the incidents which I feel might be worth a mention.

The coach really left from Glasgow but, as I was the only person from the Highlands, the tour company gave permission for me to travel by train and join the others in London.

I left a day early and stayed with cousins in Edinburgh the first night. The following evening I left Edinburgh at 11.00 p.m. and, as I had a single berth sleeping compartment, I slept all the way. I asked the sleeping berth attendant to call me at 6.00 a.m. which he did and also gave me a cup of tea and biscuits as we were approaching King's Cross.

Unfortunately, I dropped off to sleep again and woke up to find the train was stationary. After getting washed and dressed I pulled up the blind, opened the window and looked out.

31

One of the benefits to rail travellers at that time, and hardly seen today, was the railway porter always available to help with luggage. One such person was standing on the platform outside my compartment and said 'porter, Madam?' I answered 'no, thank you, I'm going to King's Cross.' He then said, 'this *is* King's Cross and all the other passengers have left the train.'

It was then 6.40 a.m. and I was supposed to be at Lyons Corner House, Buckingham Palace Road at 6.30 a.m. for breakfast. However, despite the fact that it was August Bank Holiday week-end I managed to get a taxi and eventually reached the restaurant where a very agitated tour representative rushed me in for the quickest breakfast I have ever eaten.

We then had to walk the short distance to Victoria Station to join the train for Dover and thence the Channel crossing. During the war we had heard so much about the 'bluebirds over the white cliffs of Dover'. I had looked forward to seeing the sparkling white cliffs under a blue sky as I stood at the rail watching the receding coastline. So much for my imagined picture! The reality was vastly different.

We could hardly see the white cliffs as we left them because of thick fog in the Channel. We all sat, feeling frozen and miserable, while we ate our packed lunch which had been supplied by the restaurant. The lunch was very good and I think in a way it compensated for the cold, miserable crossing.

By the time we reached Ostend the fog had cleared and the sun shone as I stepped on foreign soil for the first time.

There was an elderly lady on the quay who came to talk to us. She told us she married a Belgian gentleman just after the First World War and quite often met the boats from England. I don't know the reason but she may have been homesick and meeting British people may have helped a bit.

After we left Ostend we took the autobahn to Brussels and on to Hans-sur-Lesse in the Belgian Ardennes where we spent our first night. There was a slight hitch as we sat down to dinner. The lights failed due to a power cut so we ate by candlelight which was rather nice.

The part of Belgium which we travelled through was mainly agricultural and similar to Highland crofting land with each farmer having a tiny bit of land where they grew a little of each crop, probably just sufficient for the family.

The harvest was being cut, mostly by scythe, and the womenfolk, some quite old and all dressed in black, were tying the sheaves. Nearly everyone had a few sheep and one or two cows tethered by the roadside.

Nowadays, when I see people entering or leaving tour coaches I feel tremendous admiration for the way they are able to cope with moving from one hotel to the other and spending hours on the road. I forget I did exactly the same thing nearly thirty years ago.

We stopped overnight at two different hotels, one at Hans-sur-Lesse and the other at Heppenheim before reaching our final destination at Kisslegg, a lovely German village in Upper Suabia at the centre of the wine producing country.

We had a Hungarian courier and a Belgian driver, each in his own way responsible for making our holiday so successful. At one point, however, our driver became too enthusiastic to reach our next stop and was flagged down by the German police on the autobahn. The courier told us afterwards he was doing 85 m.p.h. when the speed limit was 60 m.p.h. for coaches. Perhaps if she had known, my mother may have felt the holiday in Norway would have been safer after all.

I should like to offer a piece of advice to would-be holidaymakers who plan to take shortcuts when writing postcards. I think nowadays the flood of holiday postcards has been reduced to a trickle but in the fifties one was always expected to send to family and friends.

Here is the way I made the mistake. Our first stop for shopping was in Luxemburg City where we got our German currency as we were advised by the courier we would get a higher rate of exchange there. I decided to get the postcard business over and done with as soon as possible so bought three dozen cards and stamps at the same time.

I kept about a dozen cards to send to family and the others were for friends. When we reached our final destination at Kisslegg we had more free time so one evening I started the project. I wrote the same message on each card and then copied the addresses from my address book. I systematically went through the book and the cards were done quite speedily. It wasn't until after the holiday when I met two friends with the same surname that I realised my mistake. One said, 'thank you for the postcard – in fact two postcards from the same place and with the same message.' The other friend said, 'thank you for the postcard which

33

I haven't received yet.' We are all still friends and laugh about the postcard business to this day.

There were many firsts for me during this holiday. It was the first time I crossed the English Channel and travelled in foreign countries. There was the first time I saw vineyards which were always on the sunny slopes and ran right down to the roadside. I was both interested and impressed to see row upon row of vines which were obviously so carefully tended. I am no connoisseur but to this day I prefer German wine to that from any other country. Did my first sight of a vineyard have anything to do with it, I wonder?

I do not have fond memories of my first, and, as it happens, my last, wine-tasting: quite the reverse in fact. The proprietor of the hotel in which we stayed in Kisslegg was also a well known wine merchant and one evening we were invited to visit his wine cellars. The son of the house accompanied us and explained the whole process of wine making.

The barrels were huge and the cellars were cold, damp places. We were each given a glass before the wine tasting started. I sometimes watch a TV programme where the experts taste and spit out the wine. I feel that, on the night in the German wine cellar, I made the mistake of swallowing too much and not spitting out enough.

Much to our surprise, in Germany we were given full cooked English breakfast instead of the usual Continental one consisting of croissants and coffee. The morning after the wine tasting I couldn't even look at the breakfast table. There were two ladies, however, who proved to be very helpful. They were sisters and at that time I thought they were elderly but they were probably middle-aged.

Unlike me, I think they came on holiday prepared for any emergency. They really were amazing and no matter what went wrong they had the remedy for it, whether it was needle and thread for a loose button or an item from their well equipped first aid box. In my case it was a mixture for the 'morning after', something which I am perfectly sure would never be required by either of the ladies. I was very grateful, however, as we had a long day ahead of us and I did not want to miss any of it.

After leaving Germany we travelled through part of Austria and then into Switzerland where we stopped for shopping at St. Gallen, a lovely market town. There was a large open fruit and vegetable market and we all did some shopping there. I think I was looking ahead when I, along with several other women in our party, bought some gorgeous Swiss chocolate, a real luxury at that time.

After leaving St. Gallen we went to Schwagalp where we had our packed lunch before taking the cable car up Santis Mountain in the Swiss Alps. It truly was, for me, one of the highlights of the tour and by lunchtime the mixture must have worked its magic so I was able to enjoy the remainder of the day.

I had never been in a cable car, nor even seen one before that day so I was rather wary at first. However, as the car moved up the side of the mountain it was the most marvellous experience and one I shall always remember. Although there were about thirty people in the cable car there was no chattering as usually happens when a crowd of people get together: I think we must have been either very moved or petrified. We could see climbers who were making the journey on foot and appeared as tiny dots on the side of the mountain.

The view from the top was magnificent and we could see right across to Lake Constance in the distance. We really felt as if we were on top of the world and the Swiss gentleman, in his *lederhosen*, playing the alpenhorn at the summit was quite striking, even though his knees may have been rather cold.

After leaving Santis we travelled to the Principality of Liechtenstein, one of the smallest independent states in the world. It seems a tremendous amount of travelling to do in one day but it really was one of the most enjoyable days of our tour.

The courier gave us some facts about Liechtenstein which I shall now relate. They may not be the same today but when we heard them nearly forty years ago we thought it seemed like paradise on earth.

Liechtenstein is just under sixty-one square miles and is the last German speaking monarchy in existence. There was no poverty, no unemployment, no exchange control and even the Customs was handled by the Swiss. The police force consisted of twelve men and a dog and was concerned mainly with traffic problems as crime was rare – in fact, although they had a prison it was very rarely used. I wonder if life is still as idyllic for the people of Liechtenstein.

We spent some time in Vaduz, the capital, with its fairy-tale castle perched high up overlooking the town. I bought a pale lemon pure silk square with sprays of alpine flowers printed on it. It was a real luxury so soon after wartime austerity and I wore it with pleasure for many years.

When we had done our shopping we all sat outside at tables and were served with icecream or iced drinks. The weather was not extremely hot but just pleasantly warm for sitting out or travelling by coach and admiring the beautiful scenery.

After leaving Liechtenstein we again crossed a corner of Austria to reach Germany and then on to our hotel in time for dinner. We all agreed it had been an exceptional day which was enjoyed by all. It was also a very long day out so no sleeping tablets were required that night.

I think some days in the tour stand out in the memory more than others. One of those was when we went to Austria by the German Alp Road, the road which Hitler had built so that, if he lost the war he could use it to get to Lindau and escape to Switzerland.

When we reached Austria we first visited Obersdorf, centre of the Championship Ski Jumping Competitions and from there went to the Little Walser Valley. I thought Austria the loveliest of all the countries were visited. We stopped at Hirschegg where we had tea and *gâteau* (quite scrumptious) before taking the chair-lift to the top of the small mountain, not nearly so high as the Swiss mountain. Although I used the Aviemore chair-lift at a later date my first venture by ski-lift was in Austria. I still clearly remember the alpine flowers and the silence broken only by the sound of the cow bells in the distance.

I sometimes think I would like to return to the countries we visited but it might spoil the image I have retained of peace and beauty. I was there before the tourist trade really got under way and the countries may be quite different today. I do not mean spoiled in any way, but in having to cater for many more holiday people they may now be different.

Our last night in Germany was spent at Coblenz, in a hotel right up on a cliff overlooking the Rhine. The view from the hotel was breathtaking and at night we thought there was a firework display in our honour. However, we realized almost immediately that it was lightning which was spectacular as we viewed it from the comfort of the dining room. It was quite an impressive ending to our German holiday.

After we left Coblenz we went to Bonn and then on to Cologne where we visited the cathedral and the 4711 shop, the makers of eau-de-cologne. Cologne was the only place where we saw bomb damage and also bullet damage to buildings which, we were told, happened at the end of the war when the Allied forces were pushing forward towards Berlin.

Afterwards, we crossed the border into Holland where we stopped at Maastricht. I wish my memory was clearer as the town is so much in the news at the present time. All I do remember is having tea for the first time in a Chinese restaurant there. Our holiday was called 'The Six Countries Tour' and Holland was one of the six. All we saw was a tiny part and Maastricht happened to be the only town: no clogs, no windmills, no blue and white delft-ware.

Our last night on the continent was spent at Blankenberge and the following morning we left for Ostend where we caught the ferry for Dover. I have just been reading something Nancy Mitford said when she lived in Paris, 'when I left Dover it was freezing cold and pouring with rain, and then, suddenly, halfway across the Channel, with France in sight, the clouds would part and out came the sun.' Unfortunately it didn't happen that way for me as there was fog in the Channel again on our return trip so I never really saw the white cliffs.

CHAPTER 5

By the early sixties all the fledglings had left the nest so mother and I were left on our own.

A few years previously I had applied for a position as a Civil Servant and, because of my health record, I was more or less told I could have the job so long as I remained healthy. As it happened, I remained in the service for over thirty years until I retired. During that time I sometimes met colleagues, supposedly on sick leave, doing their shopping but they did not have the threat of dismissal hanging over them because of ill-health. I always found it mildly amusing and thought of the troubled conscience we hear so much about nowadays.

In the same year I sat and passed the Civil Service exam I also passed my driving test. I was, I suppose, typical of the women drivers beloved by comedians. In my case, on my first test I was told to turn right at a certain roundabout. During my lessons I had never driven in that part of town but that, of course, was no excuse for my blunder. I certainly did turn right but omitted to change down so went round in top gear, just missing a stationary lorry which was wrongly parked beside the last exit. The examiner, of course, was furious and quite rightly, but I felt he could have praised me a little for missing the lorry.

A friend sat her test some time later but I think her examiner came off even worse than mine. He told her, as they all do, that he would tap the window with his newspaper when he wanted her to do the emergency stop. She did not stop at the time but suddenly remembered a few minutes later, took him unawares and did the most perfect emergency stop but the examiner hit his head on the windscreen and up came a bump like an egg. He was not amused and failed her. I think men probably do just as many stupid things when learning to drive but do not admit to them. I feel one of the prerequisites for a driving examiner to qualify for the job is to have a face which, under no circumstances, will smile.

My first car, after I passed my test, was a Morris 1000 convertible. I am reminded of this nowadays because an antique dealer in a well-known TV programme owns the same type of car, only his is slightly more battered than mine and he calls his Miriam. Mine didn't have a name but I was a very proud owner, nevertheless. I think I showed off a bit because I drove around with the hood down all summer except in pouring rain. There is something very exhilarating about driving around in an open car, especially on country roads.

The Morris was two years old when I bought it but I didn't have any major problems with it. However, one morning on my way to work and, luckily, quite near the office, it suddenly stopped for no reason that I could see. It was on a side road with not much traffic but there were other drivers, like me, taking a short cut on what was really a track.

I decided to do the 'damsel in distress' bit and I think my experience in the local drama club helped because the first driver I flagged down stopped. He was a postman so I hope the mail was not too long delayed that day. He lifted the bonnet and had a look inside but could not discover what the problem was and the next Good Samaritan was just as mystified.

They decided the best thing to do was to leave the car and one of them gave me a lift to the office. I phoned a local garage who promised to tow the car in and do any repair which was required. I called at the garage at lunchtime expecting a large bill and when I asked what was wrong I was told the car had a faulty petrol gauge and it had run out of petrol.

The next time I had a problem was after it had rained heavily all day. One part of the road was notorious for flooding as a burn nearby could not cope with the extra water. I drove too quickly through the floods when giving a lift to a friend who was trying to catch a bus on the main road. After I dropped her the car started going slower and slower, then finally stopped at a very bad corner. I was lucky that the AA caravan was only about twenty yards away so I walked back and the two men returned with me - one to direct the traffic and the other to fix my car.

While this was happening a fellow member of the drama club saw my car and stopped to offer me a lift. By this time the AA men had managed to get the car started and when I was asked for my membership card my drama colleague said, 'she isn't a member – she nicked that badge on the front of her car.' I don't know whether they believed him or not, but the AA men asked me to hand in the card next time I was passing, which I did the following day.

One morning, just as I was about to leave for the office, a big Irishman arrived at the door and asked if I could give him some food. He told me he had come from Aberdeen and was on his way to Fort William to look for a job. I do not know, and he didn't say, why he left the main Aberdeen-Inverness road and walked over a mile to our cottages in search of food when there were many houses much nearer the main road. Anyhow, I made him some sandwiches and a mug of tea which he ate outside. After giving me a thousand blessings, he left.

There was an old Anderson shelter just outside our garden which had never been used as an air raid shelter during the war. When we acquired it, after the war, we used it for storing firewood and called it 'the tin shed'. My bedroom was nearest to it and sometimes at night I heard noises which I always thought were made by birds that roosted in the shed.

The night following the Irishman's visit I heard noises and couldn't sleep so crept through to my mother's room and whispered, 'the Irishman is in the tin shed.' I do not think she believed me but said I could spend the night in her room. After a while she fell asleep and started to snore loudly. I woke her up and said, 'I'm going back to my own room – I'd rather put up with the Irishman than your snoring.'

We discovered afterwards that the man had spent the night in question in a barn belonging to a local farmer and was nowhere near our 'tin shed'. I don't think he could have been in a great hurry to get to the job in Fort William as various farmers in our area found him in the morning after he had dossed down for the night in their barns. He was taking full advantage of the well-known Highland hospitality.

I mentioned previously about the wildlife in the wood which ran alongside our garden. One species of bird was the tawny owl which, although very rarely seen as it is nocturnal, we certainly heard, especially on moonlit nights. It sometimes made a hooting sound but occasionally it was a loud, shrieking noise, and we often wondered, on the nights of the shrieks, whether we were hearing the tawny owl or the barn owl. In the morning my mother, who often used Gaelic words, would say, 'did the *cailleach oichd* disturb you last night?' The English translation is 'old lady of the night', a very apt description, I think, as the owl's round face and unblinking eyes remind one of a very old lady.

About this time some of my leisure hours were spent with the local drama club and also as a member of the Civil Defence Corps. Our weekly meetings for the latter were held in an underground bunker just outside Inverness. It was well camouflaged and had been a wartime base, I understand, for the Observer Corps.

I found what we learned during our weekly meetings to be both interesting, and in a way, frightening as it had to do with the after-effects of a nuclear bomb attack. We were to be responsible for contacting all the volunteer groups who would organize aid for the local people in the, hopefully, unlikely event of a bomb being dropped.

I also, because of Civil Defence, had my one and only experience of eating and sleeping in a real castle. I joined the corps towards the end of its existence so I only took part in one week-end exercise away from home. It was at Taymouth Castle in Perthshire.

We had quite smart navy uniform during our time in Civil Defence. For ladies it consisted of skirt, jacket, beret, shoes and greatcoat. I found the shoes too heavy and hardly ever wore the coat. When, happily, it was considered a nuclear attack was unlikely the Civil Defence Corps was disbanded. We were never asked to return the uniform so mine was hanging in the wardrobe for a considerable time afterwards.

One evening when I arrived home from work my mother said, 'a poor old tramp called today and asked for clothes so I gave him your greatcoat as you never wear it anyway.' I said, 'did you take the tabs off the shoulders?' When the answer was 'no' I realized there was an old gentleman of the road tramping round the countryside with the notice on his sleeve 'Statistics and Intelligence'.

Amateur dramatic societies were still popular in the fifties and sixties because TV had not attained the popularity which it has today. We had weekly meetings and, during the winter months, rehearsed three one-act plays to be performed at a concert in March or April. It could not be any later because the windows of the local hall had no curtains so the concert had to be held during the dark evenings.

We even became competitive and took part on a couple of occasions in the old Empire Theatre in Inverness during the Scottish Community Drama Festival. I understand it is still held but on a much smaller scale. One year the date of the concert had to be changed as one of the principal actors was unavailable on the original date. He had to go to the Western Isles to help his grandfather cut the peat, something which everyone agreed was more important than a drama concert.

CHAPTER 6

In the late sixties the government decided that our department was to be centralized so I was obliged to exchange my happy rural homelife for one in a rather grey, drab industrial town in the central belt. The one bright spot was that accommodation was found for us, so my new home was in a newly built block of flats.

Some of the younger staff members from offices throughout Scotland had to live in hostels in the new town and found it difficult to adjust to the new way of life.

Quite a number of wives refused to leave their comfortable homes for the unknown and did not want to disrupt their children's education. In those cases the husbands had to make the painful decision to give up a secure position so they resigned and eventually found other jobs.

I was lucky in that I was mature and independent enough to furnish my flat and live alone for the first time in my life. I was fortunate that my flat was in a quiet, residential part of the town and my neighbours friendly. There were four flats on each floor, twelve flats in all.

One of my neighbours educated me in what was, for me, a new experience, 'doing the stairs'. I duly bought the requisite bucket and mop, as advised, and every four weeks I took my turn to wash the landing and also the flight of stairs to the ground floor.

The stairs weren't too bad but there was also the bin shelter to scrub out and both jobs had to be done at the same time. I absolutely loathed doing that bin shelter and feel the utmost compassion for the people who, year in and year out, are still slaving away doing stairs and bin shelters.

When my turn came round I tried to get it over and done with as soon as possible. My method was to sweep the floor, then stand in the doorway with the bucket full of water and a liberal quantity of disinfectant. Wellies were essential and it was rather like scrubbing the deck as I tossed the contents of the bucket to the far side of the shelter. I then swabbed the floor with the help of a hard brush. The final part of the operation was to fix each bin bag in the metal holder provided.

I then, thankfully, returned to my flat for a much needed bath and sent up a little prayer of thanks that the job was over for another four weeks. There was a plastic key put through the letter-box to remind us of our 'turn' and I hated to come home after a busy day at the office to find the dreaded key lying on the hall carpet although I had a good idea when it was due. Is there any wonder that I hated the stairs/bin shelter job?

I mentioned earlier about our uncle, my mother's only brother, who helped my mother so much when we were children. He became a widower in the early forties and a few years before I moved to the new town his only child, a daughter, died. He then sold his house and came to live with my mother and me.

I travelled to Inverness to visit them every two weeks for the first ten months and then, sadly, they both died within three weeks of each other. It was the greatest blow of my life and made more so as I was living in a strange town and far from family and friends. However, my office colleagues, new friends and especially my neighbours gave me tremendous help and support. With their assistance I managed to struggle through a very traumatic time of my life.

Our family home stood empty for over a year until my eldest sister and her husband sold their business and moved north. I felt that first year was too soon to return to Inverness on holiday so I decided to go to Ireland, a country I had always wanted to visit and to discover whether it really was the 'emerald isle'.

I made enquiries and discovered there was a holiday coach tour company in a small village by Loch Lomond. They did tours to both Northern Ireland and the Republic. I booked for the Northern Ireland tour although the final destination was Donegal in the Republic.

I had to drive to the setting off point and was putting my suitcase in my car when my next door neighbour was washing his car. When he asked me where I was going on holiday and I told him it was to Ireland he said, 'not Northern Ireland?' I then confirmed that we were to travel through Ulster and his next statement reminded me of Humphrey Bogart in the film *Casablanca*: 'Of all the places in the world for a holiday you have to choose Northern Ireland.' At that time, unfortunately, tourists avoided Ireland like the plague.

Well, despite what is commonly called 'the troubles' that was one of my best holidays ever. It certainly was not one of the cheapest but was well worth the extra cost. The people were friendly, the hotels luxurious, and the food was the best hotel food I have ever tasted.

People are always eager to give advice to those about to go on holiday. The lady who sat at the next desk to me in the office asked how much my holiday was to cost. I thought at the time it was not in the best taste to ask such questions but nevertheless I told her. She then said, 'you could have had two weeks in Majorca for that amount,' so I mentioned in the kindest possible way that Majorca was the last place I wished to visit.

I've never been a 'beach person', possibly because I cannot swim, despite the fact that my childhood summers were spent by the shores of the Moray Firth, as I mentioned earlier. My only knowledge of seaside holidays has been gleaned from TV programmes. My own opinion, for what it is worth, is of days spent lying among hundreds of other sweaty, oily bodies like human versions of seals or sea-lions.

In the evening the food is laid out for people to choose their own and I should hate to eat anything which has been breathed on by so many other people. However, thousands of tourists enjoy this type of holiday every year so I may be completely mistaken in my judgement of it.

I have wandered off the subject of my Irish holiday and now shall return to it. We travelled by coach to Stranraer where we caught the ferry which took us across the Irish Sea to Larne. One thing which struck me almost immediately we landed on Irish soil was that it really is an emerald isle.

I remembered how beautiful and green Austria was but I think Ireland would beat it hands down. It may have to do with 'the rain sweeping in from the Atlantic' as the TV weathermen are wont to say in their broadcasts. Anyway, remembering my girl guide motto I had splashed out and bought a new raincoat with matching hat so really was prepared.

We must have been one of the smallest organized coach tours. The company ran a tour to both Northern and Southern Ireland so we all spent the first night in Dunmurry just outside Belfast. The hotel was beautiful, originally the home of Barbour, the well-known linen manufacturer. The head waiter chatted to us and when we asked if the hotel had a ghost, for it was an old manor house, he said, 'I believe it has because the owld fella strung himself up in the summer house.'

The following morning, having had no night visitation by the 'owld fella', our two coaches left for different destinations. As I mentioned previously, we were a very small group on the Northern Ireland tour. We were five in all – four ladies and one gentleman. We had a driver and courier so I feel we did not add a great deal to the firm's profits.

In one of the hotels where we stayed there was another small party of people in the dining room. We were just as interested in them as they were in us. It transpired they were members of a film company making a film about an obscure Irish poet. One member of the company asked our courier if we were well known. It must have been rather disappointing to be told we were just a small group of tourists making our way to Donegal.

Our courier, although Scottish, had relatives in Ireland and, as we drove across the country she had a wealth of folk-tales to tell us. There were also tapes of Irish songs being played making our journey both interesting and entertaining.

One of the stories I particularly remember was about the two giants who had a fight. The one caught a sod of earth and threw it at the other but missed him. The spot where he picked up the turf is now Lough Neagh and where it landed in the Irish Sea it formed an island which is now the Isle of Man. We were told that if we studied the shapes of both Lough Neagh and the Isle of Man we would discover they are the same. When I examined them on a map I must admit they did not seem identical but then, they may have altered over the years. That is an example of the folklore which helped to brighten our travels across Ireland.

The scenery, too, was well worth our attention. I have always been loyal to my own country and think Scottish scenery, and especially Highland, must be among the finest in the world. I feel I am not alone in this assumption because why else would tourists journey half-way round the world to visit and admire our beautiful country? In the same way, for the same reason, I understand many more people are visiting Northern Ireland than in the early seventies. Our little group of five must have been some of the early pioneers. Perhaps when the tour operators saw how low the bookings were they decided to go ahead, nevertheless, so that we could return and tell our friends what a wonderful country Ireland really is, despite the adverse publicity it received at that time.

We stayed in three different hotels during our holiday and in each one we met many American tourists. I have always found them very friendly and talkative and mostly are quite eager to trace ancestors who had lived in Scotland before emigrating to the New World. They are also to be found near my present home where they can be seen anxiously searching for the graves of their clansmen on Culloden Battlefield.

We spent one night in an hotel in Letterkenny and here, too, there were quite a number of American guests. After dinner we were entertained by a pianist and a couple of singers. The pianist played negro spirituals for the Americans and we were honoured by having Scottish songs played but what we all really wanted to hear was Irish music and Irish songs sung by the people who knew them so well.

After leaving Letterkenny we travelled by Lough Swilly to the north and finally followed the coast road to Dungloe. It was a truly magnificent journey with huge stretches of beautiful deserted beaches and rocky coastline.

We finally reached our destination on the beautiful west coast of Ireland in the small town of Dungloe in County Donegal.

Our hotel was outside the town of Dungloe and, like the others, was very comfortable with excellent food. We travelled each day within the county of Donegal.

One day we visited Glen Colum Killie (the glen of St. Columba) where there was a folk museum. There were three cottages furnished in the traditional style of seventeenth, eighteenth and nineteenth centuries. We had tea in one of them, served on a trestle table by a lady who made scones and pancakes on a griddle, or girdle, over a peat fire. The baked items were delicious and we all enjoyed our tea.

Aran garments, knitted locally, were sold in one of the cottages. I bought a coat which has never lost its good appearance and I still wear it to this day.

Another day it was suggested we might like to take a boat trip to Aran Island, from where the knitted garments got their name. We all agreed it would be a pleasant day out and looked forward to the sail. The bus driver ran us to the landing stage and promised to return for us later in the day.

I am not the bravest person in a small boat and especially one which was to cross a stretch of the Atlantic, even if it was quite a short crossing. Somehow I imagined it would be a small ferry boat but never the tiny open boat which it turned out to be. It certainly had a motor so there was no question of us being 'rowed across the Atlantic'. We had enjoyed quite good weather since we came to Ireland but that day it was quite awful with squally showers.

There were two long wooden seats on the boat – one on either side. The intrepid five sat on one side and on the other were two ladies who were daily workers in the hotel on Aran Island. I admired their courage because they had to make the trip each day. Two friends of the boatman also sat on the opposite seat so we were ten in all. I have never experienced anything like that crossing and never wish to do so again.

The rain was really heavy once we got out into the open sea and the wind whipped up the waves so the boat bobbed up and down like a cork but, luckily, we had an expert boatman who did the trip regularly and knew the sea in all its moods. He put a tarpaulin over us to keep most of the rain out but the other passengers seemed to be quite happy sitting in the open.

Perhaps one reason for the tarpaulin was so that we could not see the height of the waves. As we approached Aran Island the boatman, with true Irish humour, lifted a corner of the tarpaulin and said, 'how are the first class passengers?'

We had large breakfasts and dinners so did not eat very much during the day. This was quite fortunate that particular day for all we wanted by the time we landed and tottered up to the hotel on the island was a cup of tea, or something stronger to steady our nerves.

The island was beautiful and despite the crossing we all agreed it was well worth a visit. The rain cleared and the wind lessened by the time we were ready to leave making our return sail to the mainland much more agreeable than on the way out.

Another day of our holiday was spent on a visit to the lovely old town of Donegal. We thoroughly enjoyed our shopping trip and arranged to meet at a restaurant for afternoon tea.

I became separated from the other members of our small party and was quite alarmed when confronted by a band of tinkers or gypsies. The men seemed quiet but one of the women was quite determined that I should cross her palm with silver and have my fortune told. I got such a fright I gave her some money and fled as quickly as possible without hearing about my future.

One of the things I had hoped to do during our holiday was have a ride in an Irish jaunting car but we did not see any and I feel they are probably to be found more in the south of the Irish Republic.

On our last day in Ireland we again stayed in the Dunmurry hotel. We were asked if we would like to attend an Elizabethan banquet in Newry which is just on the border. We all agreed and as we were such a small group we were taken by taxi and met the members of the Southern Ireland tour.

The evening's entertainment was called 'Finn McCool's Banquet' but who Finn McCool was we never found out but thought he might have been another giant in Irish folklore.

We sat at long wooden tables, ate spare ribs which were delicious and drank mead which also was rather good and which made our eyes sparkle and the whole evening extra enjoyable.

We were entertained by a singer, a comedian and some children who danced superbly. The boys in the dancing group wore beige tweed kilts and mauve jackets while the girls, who were very pretty, wore dresses in the same colours as the boys' outfits.

The whole evening was excellent and a perfect ending to our holiday. I was able to return home and tell the people in my small world that Ireland was an ideal country for a holiday.

The following year I joined my sister, her husband and their young son for a camping holiday in the Yorkshire Dales. I had camped on two previous occasions and I must say that I did not consider either of them the perfect holiday. The one was lovely during the day when the weather was warm and sunny but I kept thinking of my warm, cosy bed at home as I felt quite chilled and uncomfortable during the night. The second holiday was even worse as the rain never ceased and we had to return home earlier than expected. However, when invited to join the little group I decided to have one more go at the outdoor life.

It was easy to decide about day-time clothes but sleep-wear was more difficult to choose. I opted for comfort rather than glamour and kitted myself out as best I could with what was available. The tent was quite roomy with three compartments so I had my own small sleeping quarters.

After preparing for bed I decided to pay a last visit to the ladies' room some distance across the campsite. When my sister saw me she burst out laughing and said, 'you look like Andy Pandy', a character currently popular with her own small children. I didn't really mind what I looked like so long as I was comfortable. The Andy Pandy outfit certainly kept me warm and I slept well, quite different from my previous camping experience.

The weather was warm and sunny, ideal for our type of holiday and for enhancing the beauty of the countryside through which we travelled.

I think bacon and eggs cooked on a camp-fire taste so much better than when done on an ordinary cooker. My opinion is that any food tastes better eaten outside, whether when camping or just having a picnic. Our days spent in the pure clean air of the Dales certainly improved our appetites and my sister should have been awarded a gold star for the way she organized the catering.

On any holiday one place or incident usually stands out in the mind for a long time. In my case, on this holiday, it was the day we went to Haworth and surrounding area. Haworth is a very pretty, picturesque village and our visit to the Bronte home, the Parsonage, at the top of the hill, was the highlight of our day.

The Brontes were such an interesting, brilliant, and yet tragic family and it was marvellous to be able to wander in and out of rooms where they had actually lived during the last century. As we travelled round the wild and beautiful moorland district it was very easy to understand how Emily and Charlotte were inspired to write *Wuthering Heights* and *Jane Eyre*.

I must say I am more a warm, comfortable bed type of person rather than one who can feel happy sleeping in a camp-bed. However, I have to admit I thoroughly enjoyed the holiday and returned home with batteries recharged and able to face the prospect of spending the next few months in an unhealthy, overheated office and returning at night to an equally unhealthy overheated flat. Of course, the latter was my own fault as I should have lived with all the windows open and the heating turned down.

CHAPTER 7

My next door neighbour, who had done the Humphrey Bogart impression, decided that, as an orphan, albeit a rather ancient one, I needed someone to look after me. In 1973, therefore, I married the boy next door although we were more the Derby and Joan rather than the Jack and Jill age group.

It was the year when several well-known couples were joined in holy matrimony but, sadly, since then a few of them have parted. I do not wish to appear smug or even soppy but I really feel our marriage was made in heaven. We, of course, were not famous or well-known, except to our families and friends.

We travelled to the registry office in the same car with our two witnesses, so dispelling the myth that it is unlucky for bride and groom to see each other on the wedding day before meeting at the altar. We had issued no wedding invitations but my sister had organized a surprise reception for us when we returned to the flat after the ceremony.

She had even made a beautiful iced wedding-cake and laid on champagne for a dozen members of both families who lived nearby. We then drove out to Glasgow Airport where we had a quick lunch before our friends waved goodbye as we boarded the plane for Paris. We had a wonderful, happy day and what could compare with a champagne reception and a honeymoon in Paris?

Although it was my first visit to Paris my husband had been there on several occasions. The first time was in 1938 when, as a sixteen year old, he joined his parents on their last holiday in Europe before the war.

His mother was a teacher and also a diplomat as I shall now demonstrate. On their first night in Paris, during a motherly talk with her son, she managed to convince him that an evening spent at the *Moulin Rouge* with his parents would be infinitely more entertaining than a night on the town with some new friends he had just met and who had suggested he join them.

In this way she probably averted a straying from the straight and narrow at such an early stage in her son's life. However, having seen the *Moulin Rouge* show for myself many years later I am not sure which was the better introduction to Paris night life for a sixteen year old.

My first impression, on arriving in the city from the airport was of traffic going in all directions and at such breakneck speeds it was a miracle there were no accidents. We were relieved to finally reach our hotel after our taxi driver managed to avoid all other forms of transport by what seemed a hair's-breadth.

The hotel was small but comfortable and the food, in true French style, was superb. The staff were friendly and took an interest in our daily outings. As we were so much older than the usual newlyweds they thought we were an old married couple so we were spared the normal secret glances reserved for honeymooners.

There are several words frequently used to describe Paris, for example, charm, elegance, luxury. It may seem banal to say so but I have the feeling they are all true and yet I cannot say why this should be. The people are no more friendly than in any other city and I doubt if the buildings are superior in the architectural sense. However, the buildings in particular have a charm all their own. French women, rightly so, are noted as being the most elegant in the world and this is seen particularly in Paris. On the whole they do not seem to have a weight problem so can wear any clothes and look stunning.

I was completely bowled over by the magic of Paris and, of course, having a tall, handsome escort added to the attraction. As my husband was not a stranger to the city we were able to visit the usual well-known places without having to depend on the services of a tour guide.

We were also able, with the help of a city map, to explore little-known but just as interesting areas. Eating out is very expensive but we discovered small restaurants off the tourist route where the food was just as good at a much reduced cost.

We sat, as all tourists do, at a pavement café on the Champs Élysées and watched the world go by. We visited the Louvre and also the Jeu de Paume with reminders of Toulouse-Lautrec and other nineteenth century painters. All those visits were of interest to us but two places in particular stand out in my memory.

One day we joined a coach party and had a conducted tour of the Palace of Versailles. Over two hundred years ago Versailles must have been one of the most magnificent royal residences in the world. It became a museum under the Republic and still retains an air of great splendour.

I felt, as we travelled around the palace, that if our guide had lived during the revolution she would have been a royalist. I also thought that the majority of the people on the tour shared her abhorrence for the perpetrators of the atrocities which were committed at that time.

I found the visit to Versailles of much interest but felt a great sadness that hatred had brought the Parisian mob to the palace and so marked the downfall of the monarchy.

Two hundred years ago the people of the world would not have heard the lurid details of what was happening in France as they do today through the medium of TV and radio. The same hatred, nevertheless, is jut as prevalent within certain countries at the present time and the same excuse is given by the leaders. They say they want better conditions for ordinary people but they seem to have no qualms about murdering their own fellow countrymen and women in order to achieve their aims.

Although Versailles was the location for such murderous deeds at the end of the eighteenth century it was the setting for something completely opposite in the twentieth century when the Armistice was signed there in 1919 after the Great War.

During the thirties, because of family coffers being low, visits to the cinema were few and far between. I only saw two films: one was *The Little Princess* with Shirley Temple and I was reminded of the other on the day we visited Versailles. It was *A Tale of Two Cities* by Charles Dickens. We had reached the French Revolution during history lessons at school and my eldest sister took me to see the film when it was shown in Inverness. I must admit, although I loved history at school, and still do, for years I remembered more about the Shirley Temple film than *A Tale of Two Cities.*

I mentioned earlier about two places which I remember particularly about our trip to Paris. One was Versailles with its grandeur but also its air of great sadness.

The other location was the *Lido* where we spent an evening and which, according to the travel brochures, is the most famous night club in the world.

At that time, twenty years go, even ordinary people like us were expected to wear formal dress when attending theatre shows and night clubs. It was very exciting, therefore, to get dressed in our finery and be whisked away by taxi to dinner and the show.

The first thing that comes to mind about the *Lido* was the opulence of the foyer where the décor was a beautiful rich crimson shade which was repeated in the main part of the building.

An attendant took my modest stole, not a fur wrap which was the usual outdoor garment to be seen that evening. I think the furs were a sort of 'keeping up with the Joneses' as they were certainly unnecessary as a means to keep warm on a balmy July evening.

As we had booked beforehand we felt very important when we were escorted to a table for two where a romantic candlelit dinner was served before the show.

I do not want to detract from the impression of a sumptuous evening but as far as I can remember the dinner was not any better than the delicious meals served at our small hotel. The only difference was the setting and also the champagne, which, combined, made the meal extra special.

The only word which I feel would adequately describe the show is extravaganza. Some cabarets are slow-moving or boring in parts but here the evening went quickly with every minute enjoyable. I still have the programme and take a nostalgic look at it from time to time.

The costumes of the Bluebell Girls were gorgeous and the colours quite dazzling. Although at that time the show was considered a bit naughty because of the topless dancers no such thoughts would come to mind today as much more naked flesh can be seen on TV programmes.

When I glance at the *Lido* programme now I feel the present day dancers probably look much the same although there is a much younger Miss Bluebell pictured with them. The men's hairstyles are rather dated and also flared trousers are never seen today.

The show at the *Lido* happened to be on our last evening in Paris and it was a fitting end to our holiday.

After we returned home we came down to earth with a bump when we had a few days hard work to merge the contents of two flats into one. However, we managed to get everything arranged reasonably well and decided to sell certain pieces of surplus furniture. It was then back to work and settle into an entirely new lifestyle.

We visited London many times but our first visit, which lasted two weeks, was memorable because of certain noteworthy incidents.

We found the address of a London hotel in a well-known Sunday newspaper and, because of the description given, thought it seemed suitable. It proved we were correct in this assumption and, after a slight hitch to start with, we enjoyed our holiday there. There was a sign on the outside wall which said 'Ellen Terry lived here' so it was rather interesting to stay in the house where a well-known actress had lived.

Sometime during the first night water started to come through the ceiling of our bedroom and we assumed someone on the floor above had left a tap running and the water overflowed and seeped into our room. My husband reported it to the receptionist in the morning who said there was no other room available. My husband then asked to see the manager who wasn't any more helpful but said he would see what could be done.

My husband then said, 'I hope you will be able to arrange something for I have to leave shortly as I am due at Westminster at 10.00 a.m.' Before we left the hotel that morning a room had been found as if my magic. It was also far superior to the first one and had a balcony overlooking gardens.

The staff assumed my husband had business to attend to at Westminster and he did not discourage this idea. The real reason was we were to meet a friend who happened to be a Member of Parliament and had offered to give us a guided tour of the Houses of Parliament and then lunch in the House of Commons.

The day which had started so badly turned out to be most enjoyable and interesting. Our friend had arranged to take several of his constituents on a tour so we joined them. There were just the three of us for lunch which was delicious and afterwards we went out on the famous terrace. It was fascinating to see so many famous people whom we recognised from newspapers or TV.

We were treated with greater respect by the hotel staff because of the false impression of my husband's political involvement. This was heightened a couple of days later when our friend arranged for us to sit in the Strangers' Gallery and listen to a debate.

We were now receiving V.I.P. treatment at the hotel with much interest shown in our daily outings. We decided, therefore, not to mention that our part in the debate was as onlookers in the Strangers' Gallery.

It was while we were on holiday that there was a bomb placed in the Tower of London. In recent years, in all the hotels where we stayed, there has been a television set and radio in the bedroom but on our first visit to London this was not the case. We did not, therefore, know about the bomb until we saw it mentioned on a placard outside the newsagent's shop.

I do not remember the full details but I recollect that at least one family of tourists from abroad lost a loved one in the atrocity. It is almost impossible to find adequate words to describe the horror felt by members of the public for the people who planted that bomb and, over the years, others throughout the United Kingdom and Europe.

Our families were very concerned when they heard the news but we did not realize this until after returning home. They knew we were in London but we did not leave our address, not because it was a secret, bur rather that we did not consider it necessary. However, from then on we always left our temporary address. Our families knew we enjoyed visiting places of historical interest rather than the shops when staying in a strange city or town and they were sure the Tower would be one of them.

As a result of the bombing, people were searched before entering certain buildings. A couple of days later we decided to visit the Planetarium and Madame Tussaud's. Our first stop was the Planetarium and the search there caused my husband and me some embarrassment. I do not know if the security people are as strict today as they were then but certainly any unidentified object would have been noticed.

Like most women, I carried everything barring the kitchen sink in my handbag. I had to empty it so that it could be examined, not only by the security men but by all the people in the queue behind us. The same thing happened to all the other ladies in the queue with the same embarrassment for all husbands and partners. The procedure was repeated as we entered Madame Tussaud's where all the contents of my bag were once more put on display.

The result for me was quite a happy one. On our way back to the hotel, as we were passing a shop which sold bags, my husband said, 'don't you think it would be a good idea to carry one bag with just your purse and umbrella and leave your handbag locked in your suitcase in the hotel? Perhaps you might see a suitable bag here.' It was a sensible idea and I did buy a bag which stood me in good stead for many years to come.

The bombing of the Tower happened during our second week in London and, apart from that incident, our holiday was a very happy one. We, along with many more people, were quite determined that a crowd of monomaniacs (the only word I can think of to describe them) would not deter us from further visits to the capital city.

In my jottings I mainly mention holidays but I do not want to give the impression that our lives were one long vacation as this is far from the truth. We worked extremely hard for most of the year and we had sad times concerning family and friends.

I am convinced that the majority of people would prefer to read about happy times and funny incidents. I am reminded of words written by the American poet Ella Wheeler Wilcox:

> Laugh and the world laughs with you;
> Weep, and you weep alone;
> For the sad old earth must borrow its mirth,
> But has trouble enough of its own.

We had many short holidays in London but the first, lasting two weeks, was the longest. I shall give more details later on about further visits to London.

CHAPTER 8

My husband, a young airman, flew with Bomber Command during the last two years of World War Two. He was stationed in East Anglia and the year following our visit to London we decided to spend our main holiday in Thetford, a small town in Norfolk. We stayed at the Bell Hotel, an old coaching inn, and I used to imagine the coaches, on their way to and from London, standing there in the courtyard.

After we had booked our accommodation we discovered that the production team of the TV series *Dad's Army* usually stayed at The Bell while filming location scenes around Thetford. I wrote to John Laurie, the Scottish actor who played Private Fraser, and asked if they were likely to be there during our holidays. I had never written to any actor before then so was surprised and delighted to have a reply a few days later. Unfortunately, we did not meet the members of the cast as they were not filming until a later date but I still have the charming letter.

We motored round the area surrounding Thetford where all the old wartime airfields were once more farmland. As we drove through one village there were a few middle-aged ladies standing chatting and I said to my companion, 'they may be some of your wartime girlfriends still looking longingly for the young Scottish airman who used to whirl them round the floor in the local dance halls.'

He told me one girlfriend had made a birthday cake for him but he never tasted it for his plane was shot up over Germany. The crew all landed safely after baling out and eventually they were caught and taken to a prisoner of war camp.

This happened on my birthday in January 1945, just a few months before the war ended. Of course I did not know of this momentous happening, which took place on my birthday, until many years later.

My husband told me he landed in a wood and played hide-and-seek

63

with what seemed like the enemy counterpart of our Home Guard. I asked him how he managed to communicate when the Germans found him. He said he was too scared to say anything and just put his hands up in surrender. He was a prisoner of war for only five months and, although not too well fed, was not badly treated by his captors.

After being caught he was taken from the wood to a village for interrogation which took place in what seemed to be the village hall. As he was taken through the village the local inhabitants stood watching him, not in a hostile way but rather out of curiosity. I expect it wasn't every day that a British airman was seen in their village. They may have been thinking that the same thing could happen to their sons in Britain.

His captors took away his flying boots and replaced them with plimsolls. If it had been summer they may have been more comfortable than fur-lined boots, but Germany in January can be just as cold and frosty as Scotland. However, at least the crew were all together in the camp and a few months later were all back with their families in Britain.

It was interesting to travel through the beautiful Norfolk and Suffolk countryside and, for my husband, to revive memories of his youth.

One of the favourite haunts for young airmen in East Anglia during the war was Bury St Edmunds and we spent many happy hours there during our holiday. We enjoyed strolling along the streets of this fascinating market town which doesn't seem to have changed for centuries.

We had lunch a couple of times in the Angel Hotel where Charles Dickens stayed during the time he was giving readings in the assembly hall. We were told the Angel Hotel was the scene of Mr. Pickwick's meeting with Sam Weller in *Pickwick Papers*.

Thetford was a good central point for visiting various places of interest in that part of England. There was an excellent bus service between London and Norwich with Thetford one of the passenger pick-up points.

One day we decided to leave the car and go to Norwich by bus. We felt it would give my husband a break from driving and make the journey more interesting as we made our leisurely way through the beautiful countryside.

The bus must have been delayed somewhere between London and Thetford because it was twenty-five minutes late arriving at our stop. I think the driver had decided that, come hell or high water, he would make up the lost time so the unhurried, enjoyable run we had anticipated turned out to be more like a nightmare.

We set off, to use a well-known expression, like greased lightning and continued in that way throughout the journey. Luckily for the driver there were no police cars on the same road at that time. We even went through the small picturesque villages at top speed, only stopping now and again to pick up passengers. We were thankful to reach Norwich, and also pleased we had a different driver on the return trip so we were able to enjoy the journey back to Thetford.

We loved Norwich and thought it was one of the most beautiful and interesting cities we had ever visited.

After our hair-raising journey it was a miracle we had enough energy to walk up to the castle but were glad we did as it was well worth a visit. We also visited the cathedral with its wonderful nave roof and bosses painted with scenes from the Bible. The impressive spire must be one of the tallest in England.

Another part of Norwich we found fascinating was Elm Hill with the tree which gives the thoroughfare its name standing at the top of the cobbled street. Our time was limited so we were unable to explore that part of the city as much as we should have liked. The buildings are timber framed and pastel coloured and have a timeless quality which is quite unique. If time allowed we might have visited the interesting antique shops, pottery shops and art galleries in Elm Hill.

During our stay at Thetford we visited friends in a small village called Haddenham near Ely. It was a very hot, dry summer so all windows in the house were wide open. The ladybird is such a pretty insect it does not seem right to say there was a plague of them that year but that seems the only word to describe the invasion.

When I was a child I had often seen swarms of bees but never before a swarm of ladybirds. Our friends' kitchen was absolutely covered in ladybirds; table, working surfaces, window sills. It was the most amazing sight and the only way we could help to get them out was to use a soft brush and sweep them on to a shovel before taking them outside to gorge themselves on any greenfly available. I do not know if the problem was countrywide but I doubt if it was contained in that small part of England. I still vividly remember our visit to Haddenham and the hordes of beautiful ladybirds.

Each year we took advantage of an advertisement by a well-known hotel group offering London week-end rail inclusive bargain breaks. I have always loved rail travel and our first holiday each year became extra special when it included a journey by train plus a short visit to London.

We checked the list of theatre shows in the *Sunday Times* and usually booked a couple before our holiday. One year we could only settle upon one play and decided to have a look round the theatres after we arrived in London. We eventually bought tickets for the play *Deathtrap* at the Garrick Theatre.

I think we were about five rows from the front so had a good view of the stage. The play is well known but I shall now endeavour to explain the plot. The man who was murdered was rolled in a rug and dragged outside. The thunder and lightning which followed were very realistic. There was a huge flash of lightning and the 'dead man' suddenly appeared, large as life, standing in the doorway.

As I did not know beforehand what was going to happen I got a terrific fright and didn't realize until later that I had screamed out loud. My husband told me a woman behind us said, 'that scream took ten years off my life.' He also said other members of the audience probably thought I was put there by the producer to scream at every performance. The strange thing was, I am usually very calm and not at all the nervous, highly strung person that I seemed to be that night.

Perhaps the well-known theatre ghost had more to do with the fright than the incident in the play. Needless to say, because of the embarrassment I caused that night, our London theatre visits from then on were restricted to comedies and musicals.

On the 2nd May 1977 our journey to London was really very special but we did not know that before hand. When we arrived in Glasgow Central Station we saw the provost wearing his chain of office. There were several other important looking people beside him on the platform by the London train. We felt they could not possibly be there to wish us a pleasant journey as we had done the trip annually and nobody had bothered before then.

However, it soon became clear when we were told over the intercom that it was the Golden Jubilee run of the *Royal Scot*, which was the name of the train. All the passengers were given VIP treatment on the journey, thus making it even more enjoyable than usual. The attendants were dressed in the twenties style because the Golden Jubilee we were celebrating was 1927-1977. I still have my souvenir certificate which states 'E.C.Sherry travelled on the *Royal Scot* from Glasgow to London Euston on the occasion of the Golden Jubilee 2nd May 1977'.

On one of our London visits we were making our way to St. James's Park when the Burma Star Parade was marching from the direction of The Mall and passing Horse Guards on the way to Whitehall and the Cenotaph for their annual service. It really is very impressive to see ex-servicemen, not all too fit, marching proudly along.

They were all smartly dressed and seemed even more so compared with the down and out gentleman who had joined them and swung merrily along with his not-too-clean sleeping bag slung over his shoulder. I expect it was his sole possession and wondered if, in his prime, he had been just as smart and proud of his appearance as the men who were taking part in the parade that day. He may not have had anything to do with the Burma campaign, of course, but in his inebriated state felt it was his duty to join the other men.

I think we saw more outcasts of society like this man in London than in any other city or town we visited. I remember three of those particularly and decided, if I ever won a vast sum of money, a major part of it would go to easing their way of life. They may, of course, have been just as happy with their situation as we were with ours.

One day, being keen Conan Doyle fans, we were making our way along Baker Street when we passed what is now called a bag lady who seemed to have at least three overcoats on, and this on an extremely hot day in summer. She also had several canvas bags so had far more belongings than the man in the Burma Star Parade.

Another day we were walking along a lane somewhere near Whitehall and passing a pile of cardboard boxes when I said, 'there's a leg sticking out of that box.' On closer inspection we discovered it belonged to an old lady who was sound asleep among the boxes.

The third person I remember was an old man, also asleep, and gently snoring, lying on a park bench in the Embankment Gardens near the Savoy Hotel. We thought he possibly obtained his food supply in the waste bins belonging to the hotel. He certainly looked well-fed.

We wondered how the lives of the people just mentioned began, and when had they started on the downward slope which ended on park benches and in cardboard boxes. They must have began life in houses like everyone else so why had they ended up where they are today? To us, they have a sad tragic life, but they may now live in a fantasy world where things that seem important to us do not matter one bit to them. Things like a warm, comfortable bed, regular meals, personal hygiene do not appear to concern them and yet they manage to survive.

I have just commented on the bag ladies and their male fellow citizens and now remember other Londoners who were much higher up the social ladder.

As I mentioned previously, our London visits were made possible because of rail-inclusive bargain breaks offered by a well-known hotel group. There was a wide choice of hotels and in the seventies and early eighties we elected to say in Kensington or Bayswater. I think the latter was our favourite where we stayed several times.

The underground stations were close to both hotels so we used them frequently. We quite often caught the tube in the late afternoon from the city centre to our hotel. At that time the bowler-hatted, rolled-umbrella, city gent was making his way home after a hard day in the world of business.

Quite often we had to stand but sometimes were lucky to get a seat – in fact at that time the days of chivalry were certainly not past. If a gentleman saw a lady standing he would offer her his seat but I think the people responsible for women's lib. put a stop to all that. The male members of society probably thought, 'if they insist on equal opportunities presumably they would prefer to stand in buses and trains.'

I expect the underground trains are the same today as when we travelled on them ten years ago. Seats were quite widely spaced and passengers sat facing each other. When my husband and I were able to get seats together I usually sat by the window. When not looking out I normally glanced downwards, but not because I was shy or demure. I was, in fact, examining and admiring the elegant, expensive, hand-made shoes and especially the black silk socks which were customary footwear for the London business man. I must say, I was very discreet during the inspection and I am certain the wearer would have been unaware of it.

If I was asked to describe my fellow passengers at that time I should have found it an impossible task. I was quite ignorant regarding their appearance except for their 'pedal extremities', as a well-known American singer described them. Black silk socks have always had a fascination for me which is rather strange as I am a very ordinary housewife.

CHAPTER 9

We knew midsummer was not an ideal time for visiting London or Paris but in 1983 we arranged to have our main holiday in the two cities at the end of June and beginning of July that year. The reason for our rash decision was, our tenth wedding anniversary happened to be on the 30th June. We planned to celebrate by having a few days in London prior to leaving for Paris and our main holiday.

Our last day in London was extremely hot and in order to escape the torrid atmosphere we decided to take a boat trip to Greenwich.

The weather was perfect for a sail and so was the commentary by the young man on the boat as he described all the famous buildings which could be seen from the river. All this seems ideal but I had to devote part of my time trying to solve a ticket problem for a small foreign gentleman who happened to be sitting next to me.

He should have got off at Tower Bridge but did not discover his mistake until well past that landing stage. He told me he was a chartered accountant but I felt sorry for his clients as he seemed unable to work out the amount he owed the boat company for the extra distance. It was quite sad that neither of us were able to convince him that he had not committed a crime.

I had a feeling it was more of a molehill than the mountain he made it out to be. Perhaps in his own country the law was stricter about such matters. However, by the time we reached Greenwich we managed to solve the ticket problem.

Perhaps he lost his nerve as we approached the Tower when our guide mentioned the people who sailed to Traitor's Gate and thence to their death in the Tower.

We had only a very short time at Greenwich but it enabled us to see the Cutty Sark, the old tea-clipper. What stories it could tell of its voyages to the East! We also saw Gypsy Moth IV which seemed far too small to have sailed round the world. What a very brave man Sir Francis Chichester must have been!

The morning after our Thames boat trip we left Victoria on the train for Folkstone where we caught the cross channel ferry to Boulogne. Twenty-five years before, when I crossed the Channel for the first time, the fog was so thick I could not see the white cliffs. This crossing was quite different, with blue sky and calm sea, which made the sail very pleasant.

At Boulogne we boarded the Paris Express, a train which is smooth and fast. It was wonderful to see the French countryside as we sped through towns and villages.

Our compartment was quite long, with very comfortable seats which made the journey more pleasant. Some of our fellow passengers were French schoolboys who, we thought, were returning home after an organized school trip to Britain.

From time to time during the journey there was a mini invasion of giggling little girls who jumped on the boys' knees, kissed them and then disappeared back to their own compartment. We presumed they had met the boys prior to boarding the train. The girls returned a few times but were so pretty and attractive they would be forgiven by the other passengers for all the noise they made on the journey.

We were amused when we finally reached the Gare du Nord and all passengers left the train. The schoolgirls were met by their parents and were so quiet and demure it was a complete contrast to their behaviour on the Paris Express. The saying 'butter would not melt in their mouths' would have fitted the occasion perfectly.

On our first trip to Paris we stayed at a small family hotel which was comfortable and the food excellent. It was not, however, located in the sort of area where one could stroll around in the evening. We decided, therefore, as this was a special occasion, to have a complete contrast and 'see how the other half lives'.

We booked through the Paris Travel Agency and stayed at the Hôtel Concord Lafayette which was at the Porte Maillot near the Bois de Boulogne. The hotel was in the Palais des Congrès where there were two restaurants, a couple of theatres and eighty boutiques on two levels. The boutiques belonged to the famous Paris fashion houses so the garments sold there were well outside my price range.

Still, I enjoyed wandering round, admiring the exquisite window displays while my husband sat quite happily in the comfortable reception area. There was a pavement coffee shop where we could sit and watch the world go by.

We spent our first day getting to know our temporary home and were charmed by the sheer luxury of it all. We took the lift to the hotel roof garden with its tubs of flowers, shrubs, and a beautiful magnolia tree in full bloom. From here we had magnificent views over Paris.

I am inclined to think that no matter how many times one visits Paris its charm and magic will always be the same. Even the light over the city is remarkable, giving a softness and mystical quality. It is easy to understand why so many famous painters found it the ideal place to work. I often think, how very sad that, because of dedication to their art, the majority lived in dire poverty and yet their paintings fetch vast sums today.

We discovered, by trial and error, that the most economic means of transport was the underground. We bought seven day tourist tickets (called, appropriately Sesame) which gave us unlimited travel both on the Métro and on buses. We were then quite independent and were able to explore areas away from the normal tourist routes.

The first day we spent finding our way around the immediate surroundings. On the next couple of days we revisited both the Louvre and Jeu de Paume, where we had gone ten years before but wanted to see the wonderful paintings again.

Another day we had a complete contrast when we travelled to the Flea Market at St-Ouen, famous throughout the world. We were fascinated by everything – the items for sale, the stall-holders, and also the people wandering around looking for bargains. We had been warned about pick-pockets but were not troubled by any that day.

One day we made a sentimental journey back to the Hôtel Montholon where we stayed on our honeymoon. We walked past the hotel but were not sure if it was open to non-residents so found a small restaurant nearby where we enjoyed a delicious lunch. Although the Concorde Lafayette was more comfortable and luxurious the cuisine was no better than what we enjoyed at our first small hotel.

On our way back to our own hotel we were leaving the Métro and travelling up in the crowded escalator when there was a slight incident. My husband and I were standing on one step and on my left was a young man who seemed impatient as he was walking upwards while the other passengers were crowded on the stairs.

When he was level with us he dropped something, bent to pick it up and his head pushed against my leg. My husband became concerned but I assured him everything was all right when the young man charmingly apologized, 'Pardon, Madame'.

When we left the Métro, instead of entering the hotel we decided to have a walk in the Bois de Boulogne which was nearby. We went there most afternoons as we found it cool and peaceful after the heat and bustle of the city.

On this particular day we decided to take the miniature railway— both to rest the tired feet and see more of the park. I feel forest, rather than park, might be a better description of the Bois de Boulogne as it covers such a vast area.

When my husband was about to pay for our tickets he discovered the hundred franc note (about £10 at that time) which he knew was in his pocket, was no longer there.

We then realized what had happened on the Métro and we were told afterwards that the crooks operate in threes. One goes ahead, the second creates a diversion and the third, on the lower step, helps himself to the money. It also dawned on us that having money in trouser pockets may be all right at home but not on a crowded underground in a foreign city.

The strange thing was, we were warned about pickpockets at the Flea Market and were extra careful. We expected the people concerned would be shabbily dressed and were stealing in order to eat. Could anyone imagine that a thief would have such charming manners and appear to have as his outfitter a top Paris couturier?

We thought it best not to dwell too much on what had happened but continue to enjoy our little expeditions each day. We were, however, extra careful and there was no more change kept in trouser pockets. Anyhow, our particular robber could not have got far on £10.

We had deliberately chosen what was called a 'do it yourself' holiday. The Paris Travel Agency arranged our travel and hotel booking but we were free to do as we pleased during our stay. We found this much more relaxing than having guided tours throughout our holiday.

To celebrate our wedding anniversary my husband booked a table at the *Moulin Rouge* for a champagne dinner and cabaret. We had looked forward to our evening entertainment and were not disappointed. Our fellow dinner guests were friendly and, being American, were not so reserved as British people in telling their life stories to complete strangers.

On my left was a young Jewish law student with his maternal grandmother. She was taking him on a European tour as a graduation present. He told us about his father's family who lived in pre-war Germany. His father, who was a little boy when the war started, was taken to England by his mother but his father (the young man's grandfather) did not manage to escape. The family never heard of him again so presumed he died in a concentration camp.

Our friend's father and grandmother eventually travelled to America where many of their relatives now live. It is only when we hear of such tragedies we remember the evil of the holocaust and the anguish of the Jewish people.

On my husband's right there was another American couple – this time husband and wife. The husband was in the American Air Force during the war and was stationed in Scotland for some time. The two men swapped war-time stories during dinner. It was all the more interesting for them as they had both been air-crew.

It may seem sombre subject for discussion during a dinner which was to celebrate such a happy occasion, both for us and also the young student, who may now be a top American lawyer. At the time, however, we found the conversation interesting and we all chatted throughout the meal as if we had known one another all our lives.

Our young dinner companion told us he and his grandmother attended the cabaret at the *Lido* a couple of nights before but said they preferred the show at the *Moulin Rouge*. I think it became better known because of the film made depicting the life of Toulouse-Lautrec. The French Travel Agency, the year we were in Paris, used his drawings of the artistes for their travel brochure.

The whole entertainment was spectacular and our only regret was the evening passed too quickly. The colours of the costumes were dazzling, especially those worn in the grand finale, when the dancers looked exquisite in rose pink and white.

I have been re-reading the programme and discovered a few interesting facts. 'On October 6th 1889 a new thrill was created in Paris and the spectators making their way towards the *Moulin Rouge*, bearded men in top hats, pretty women and girls in the bloom of youth, high society and professional revellers, had scarcely any inkling of it'. This 'new thrill', whose appearance was welcomed in these terms by the novelist Armand Lanoux, was the quadrille, described as naturalistic or realistic, which the founder of the 'Bal du Moulin Rouge' launched at the same time as his establishment. This was an idea of genius, for the quadrille, which has become the French cancan, is linked for ever with the celebrated mill.

From the seventeenth to the beginning of the nineteenth century there were thirty windmills. By the nineteenth century there were no more than fifteen which were used to grind corn and press grapes. But already the far-seeing millers were turning them into places of pleasure. The 'pleasure' enjoyed there last century was not nearly so innocent as in places like the *Moulin Rouge* today.

A 'grand Gala' was held to celebrate its ninetieth birthday and many well-known international stars took part for the benefit of UNICEF.

In November 1981 the *Moulin Rouge* closed its doors for one night. The cast was invited to perform in London for Queen Elizabeth II, a great honour for them.

The opening night of the revue we saw, *Femmes, Femmes, Femmes,* was honoured with the presence of Princess Anne, and was held for the benefit of different childrens foundations.

What a delight it was for us to celebrate our anniversary in a place where so many famous people had been entertained.

During our holiday *Swan Lake* was being performed by the Paris Opera Company in one of the theatres within the hotel complex. We decided to spend our last evening at the ballet. We did not have to worry about transport and after dinner walked to the theatre without even having to go outside the building.

We had been to many theatres throughout Britain but never one so large. For us, it was a 'once in a lifetime' experience to see *Swan Lake*, or *Le Lac des Cygnes*, as it was that night, performed by a world famous company. What a superb ending to our holiday!

The following year our main holiday was spent in Shetland, a place we had always wanted to visit. We stayed with my sister and her husband who lived a short distance from Sumburgh Airport, where my brother-in-law was employed.

We drove to Inverness, left our car there and flew to Shetland. We left Inverness in sunshine and the pilot seemed to follow the coastline to the north of Scotland. We then crossed the Pentland Firth and landed for a brief stop in Orkney to pick up passengers. Between Orkney and Shetland we had to climb above the clouds because of bad weather. After the grey skies it was like entering another world with brilliant blue sky overhead and clouds which looked like huge stretches of cottonwool beneath us.

As we flew over the lighthouse prior to landing at Sumburgh the storm clouds cleared and the sun shone to welcome us. People may imagine, because there are very few trees on Shetland, that it is a bleak, barren land but this is certainly not the case. It must be one of the loveliest parts of the British Isles.

We hired a car and after a few days introduction by my sister and her husband to Mainland, as it is called, we set off each morning to explore and enjoy the beautiful countryside.

One day, we were driving north to Lerwick and passed a rather pathetic little group. Three very young schoolchildren, satchels on their backs, were standing looking down at a cat which had just lost its ninth life, probably hit by a car. They weren't talking as we drove past, just standing silently as if paying homage. Their expressions were so sad we wondered if the victim belonged to one of them.

I mentioned earlier in my jottings that I could never be the intrepid sailor in a small boat. One day, however, I decided to make an effort to overcome my fear so that we could visit the bird sanctuary of Noss, the small island famous for its bird cliffs. The boat which took us to Noss from Lerwick was slightly larger than the small open craft in Northern Ireland and at least it had a cabin to keep us reasonably dry from the salt spray.

It is doubtful if the boatman's profits would have increased on our trip as there was only one other couple and ourselves on board. We were lucky that our fellow travellers were amateur ornithologists from the north of England and were able to identify the various seabirds we spotted during our sail. The 'twitchers', as bird watchers are called nowadays, told us they spent all their holidays visiting places where unusual and interesting birds can be seen. Now, this *is* dedication to one's hobby!

On our way to Noss our friends told us the gannet, the largest British seabird, is easily recognizable by its size and also by black wing-tips and yellow patch on the head. We were delighted to see several of those birds and amazed at their huge wing-span, well over a metre. They seemed to glide effortlessly in the strong winds and then dive at great speed right into the sea and emerge with a fish.

We saw something, new to us, which seems to happen frequently in the northern waters. A brown bird, smaller than the gannet but heavily built, appeared suddenly and kept diving on the gannet until it disgorged its catch. We were told it was a great skua and its victims were usually terns and gulls who, eventually, after some dive bombing, are forced to give up their catch. We were surprised the gannet yielded so quickly as it was much bigger than the skua. I suppose, to quote Tennyson, it is another case of 'Nature, red in tooth and claw'.

We had seen TV programmes showing birds nesting on sea cliffs but were not prepared for the amazing spectacle seen from a small boat which brought us fairly close to the island.

The cliff seemed as high as a steeple and, with the help of powerful binoculars, we could see the birds nesting on narrow horizontal ledges. It appeared impossible for eggs and finally young chicks to survive in such a place, especially when they must have been buffeted by high winds and rain. There were kittiwakes on the lower ledges and guillemots above.

I must have found my sea legs that day because I really enjoyed our trip, despite being tossed about on a very rough sea. I have the feeling we were all very confident because we knew the boat was in the capable hands of an expert boatman.

One morning, complete with picnic lunch, we set off for Jarlshof, which is situated on the south of Shetland, and not far from where we stayed.

In all our wanderings over the years this must have been the most fascinating place we ever visited. Before we left home a friend lent us a book on Jarlshof so we studied it before our holiday and were allowed to take the book with us for reference.

One of the most remarkable things about this prehistoric site is, neither we nor anyone else would have seen it were it not for violent storms at the end of last century. After several of these storms had raged against the island, sections of huge stone walls were exposed and afterwards the archaeological work began. Over the years various settlements have been discovered dating from 2000 B.C. to the Middle Ages.

The last building to be erected was in the seventeenth century. This was Jarlshof, or Laird's House, the laird at that time being Earl Patrick Stewart who also owned Scalloway Castle which we visited another day. According to the dictionary, Jarl is 'an earl; a Scandinavian chief' so the name probably has Norse origins. As Jarl is earl I presume 'hof' is house, so making it 'Earl's House'.

I am always amazed at the brilliance and patience of archaeologists. They spend days, months, and sometimes years sifting through what, to we ordinary mortals, is a load of rubble and yet they come up with the most astonishing results.

In the case of Jarlshof, it was established the people occupied the village settlements from 2000 B.C. and lived and worked just as people do today. There must have been architects then, as there are now, because someone had to plan the buildings with tremendous care and attention to detail. How else could the stone walls have survived to the present day?

We had a strange feeling of unreality when we stood in rooms and walked from house to house as people had done four thousand years ago. We wondered what they looked like and how they communicated: certainly not in English as it is spoken today. They probably managed quite happily without 'mod.cons.' and yet if we have a power cut or if the central heating breaks down we think the end of the world has come.

Our Shetland holiday was certainly a memorable one, and our visit to Jarlshof quite special.

Shetland has been on the world news recently because of the *Braer* oil tanker disaster. We were very sad for the friendly people of Shetland that a tragedy so immense should have shattered their lives. We also thought of how we wandered along the beautiful clean sandy beaches with only seals and seabirds for company.

However, just as the violent storms last century brought to light the Jarlshof, the great storms this year dispersed some of the oil and, hopefully, things will return to normal in the future.

I am now going to describe the holidays we enjoyed at the opposite end of the British Isles. For several years before we retired we travelled to the south coast of England and spent a couple of weeks each year on the Sandbanks Peninsula, between Poole and Bournemouth.

We stayed at the Haven Hotel for the first two years. Marconi stayed there at the beginning of the century when he was doing his wireless telegraphy experiments. There is a Marconi lounge in the hotel. The Haven is right beside the car ferry which crosses to the Isle of Purbeck in Dorset and very convenient for us as Dorset, I think, was our favourite English county.

After the first two years at the Haven we rented a flat, also in Sandbanks, with magnificent views overlooking Poole Harbour, the second largest natural harbour in the world.

The world power-boat race happened to be staged during our second stay at the Haven Hotel. There were crowds of people watching the race and we were lucky, along with other guests, to see it from the comfort of the sun lounge which stretched the full length of the hotel front. It was very exciting to see the powerful boats leaping out of the water with such great speed.

The Italian team won that year and they, also, stayed in the Haven. It was interesting for us to share the dining-room that evening with such well-known people as they celebrated their victory.

We used the car-ferry most days and so were able to reach many places of interest to us without too much travelling. Dorset has an old-world charm which is very attractive and the villages and peaceful countryside are a joy to visit.

Our first stop after crossing by ferry was Corfe Castle, an unusual name for a village. The castle itself, which stands high above the village, was demolished by Cromwell and has remained a ruin to the present day. There is a model village and gardens just off the main street and the miniature castle is built as the original would have looked before its destruction. Corfe Castle is a lovely tranquil village, with its stone cottages which gives the impression of having been there since the beginning of time.

The Elizabethan manor house was once owned by the Bond family and we were interested to know that Bond Street in London was called after them.

A couple of times we visited the Blue Pool near Wareham. Once it was just a hole where clay had been extracted but people with imagination transformed it into a tourist attraction. The pit was flooded and a woodland created around it. Its attraction is that, depending on the weather, the water can turn either vivid blue or deep turquoise. I do not know the reason but it appears to have something to do with the clay foundation.

Country churches, with their lych-gates, are always interesting and family history can be traced by studying gravestones.

We visited the lovely Norman church at Winfrith and were particularly interested in two plaques inside the church. They were placed there in memory of a local family who lived at the beginning of the last century. There were seven children, five of whom died in infancy. One girl lived until she was fourteen and the remaining son died at twenty-six. The whole family was wiped out in less than thirty years. There were several thatched cottages in the vicinity and we wondered if they had lived in one of them.

Dorchester must be one of the county towns in Britain with the most varied stories of historical interest connected with it. Its most famous son was Thomas Hardy and one of his best known novels *The Mayor of Casterbridge* was set in the town where Hardy's statue stands today.

We paid many visits to Dorchester and always had tea at a small seventeenth century tea-room called The Napper's Mite. At first we thought a napper was a tradesman but discovered the building was originally called Napier's Almshouses, or Napper's Mite. It was founded by Sir Robert Napier in the seventeenth century to provide lodging for 'ten poor men'. Today it is a tea-room and tables are set out in a small courtyard where tea can be served, weather permitting.

The first time we were in Dorchester we bought a couple of postcards to send home. I remembered seeing the post office in the High Street so, after tea in the Napper's Mite, we made our way there. My husband stood by the window and wrote the cards while I went to the counter for stamps. We were surprised that there were no other customers as the town was busy.

I said, 'two second class stamps, please' and the man behind the counter said, 'pardon?' I thought I had spoken quite clearly so I held up two fingers and said, '*two* second class stamps, please.' The counter assistant (really a teller) then said in no uncertain terms, 'Madam, this is the National Westminster Bank and we are about to close.'

I wished at that moment that I could sink through the floor. I felt even more humiliated when my husband said I had made a rude sign in holding up two fingers, but I reminded him that Winston Churchill had made the V sign the same way. I was then informed that Churchill held his fingers in a different way. It showed how naive I was and, for my age, so ignorant about the ways of the world.

We discovered that the post office was further down the street from the bank. Our one consolation was, our financial affairs were not dealt with by that particular bank so there was no occasion for us to enter the premises again. Our friends laughed when we told them about the incident but I wonder what the bank employees thought of the rude Scotswoman who expected to buy postage stamps in their establishment.

In the seventeenth century Judge Jeffries held his notorious 'Bloody Assize' in Dorchester when he tried nearly three hundred local men for treachery after the Monmouth Rebellion. Seventy-four of the men were hanged. The occupant of Hangman's Cottage, which still stands, must have been a busy man. It is believed Judge Jeffries lodged in a house in the High Street where his ghost is supposed to appear. Does his guilty conscience not allow him to rest in peace, I wonder?

Another trial, but not nearly so appalling, happened last century when six agricultural workers were sentenced to transportation when they tried to form a trade union and requested higher wages for farm-labourers. They were later pardoned, but are still known as the Tolpuddle Martyrs. We drove through the village of Tolpuddle on our way back to our holiday home just to see where the Martyrs had lived.

I mentioned the Napper's Mite in Dorchester where we often had tea. We also enjoyed afternoon tea and lunches in the sixteenth century Marigold Cottage which is in a small picturesque village whose name escapes me but I have fond memories of the marvellous home baking and delicious lunches which we enjoyed. There was a list of all the kings and queens who reigned in England during the life of the cottage.

The ladies' toilet was in a building adjacent to the main door but we could not see facilities for gentlemen. When my husband asked the waitress about it she said, 'it's under the pear tree in the garden.' This really was the case but it was in a building, not an open-air convenience as it at first seemed.

Each year, while on holiday at Sandbanks, we re-visited Marigold Cottage and enjoyed the wonderful cuisine. We tried to imagine what the original owners looked like and also the way of life there so many centuries ago. We felt the cottage itself would not have changed much and may have started its existence much as it is today, with its whitewashed walls and thatched roof.

In the course of our travels the places which appealed most were the towns and villages in Dorset where time appears to have stood still for centuries. They were especially attractive to us at a time when we lived in an industrial town where the trauma of present day life was ever with us. The peace and tranquillity during our holidays were greatly appreciated.

In 1986, during our last stay at Sandbanks, we decided to pay our first visit to Salisbury. When wandering round towns or cities for the first time I always prefer to see buildings of historical interest rather than modern shopping precincts which, as a woman, probably makes me unique.

We decided to leave the car and use public transport so that we could both enjoy the journey through beautiful countryside. One of the villages we travelled through was Ringwood, which was of especial interest to me as my mother lived there as a young girl at the beginning of the century. The journey from Bournemouth to Salisbury took an hour and we enjoyed the leisurely trip. The driver appeared to know many of our fellow passengers who seemed to be regular travellers.

We went to Salisbury on the Monday and found it so fascinating we paid a second visit on the following Friday. It must be one of the most beautiful cities in England and we made a point of reading as much as possible about it before our second visit.

We discovered that the original castle and cathedral were built on a hill, now called Old Sarum. This site was abandoned in the thirteenth century when the new town, called New Sarum, now Salisbury, was started.

St. Thomas's Church was the first building in the new city. We were lucky to meet a clergyman in the church who very kindly gave us a guided tour and also briefly explained the history of the church. We were intrigued to discover that the city was built round the church and not, as happens today, when a church is built after a new town is established.

We were told that St. Thomas's started as a wooden chapel for the workmen who were building Salisbury Cathedral, which, incidentally, took thirty-eight years to complete. Religion, of course, would have played a greater part in people's lives in those days than it does now.

We were particularly interested in the Doom Painting, which each year is photographed by tourists from all over the world. It was painted in the fifteenth century and is said to be the largest wall-painting of the Last Judgement in existence. In order to protect it after the Reformation it was covered in whitewash and stayed that way until early last century. During re-decoration some traces of colour were noticed on the wall and, eventually, it was carefully restored.

We were fortunate, on our first trip to Salisbury, to meet a local couple with whom we shared a table during lunch and we found they were very knowledgeable about the history of the city. We enjoyed their company and were fascinated to discover the names of famous people who had stayed there at various times throughout the centuries. It is always good to meet people who take such an interest in their own locality and we were grateful to our new friends for their information.

We were told that Handel gave his first concert in England in a room over St. Ann's Gate in the famous Close. Izaak Walton, author of *The Compleat Angler*, stayed in the Close while visiting his son who was a canon of the cathedral. We wondered if the famous author spent many happy days with his rod on the banks of the River Avon. The house where he stayed is called Walton Canonry and it was there that John Constable lived while doing his famous paintings of Salisbury

Cathedral. Those are just a few of the famous people connected with the city.

I have always been fascinated by the names of inns and public houses: familiar titles such as Rose and Crown, Pig and Whistle, King's Head, King's Arms, Peacock Inn, but never, until we visited Salisbury, the Haunch of Venison. My enquiring mind wants to know why the names were chosen in the first place and how many different ones exist throughout Britain.

We enjoyed walking along the city streets and admired the varied forms of architecture seen in the buildings, the age of which spans several centuries. The roofs are a warm red shade and there are many timbered houses, also shops with bow windows. Some of the half-timbered buildings date back to Tudor times and, I feel sure, look much the same today as they did four hundred years ago.

The Poultry Cross in the High Street is fourteenth or fifteenth century and we were given three versions of how it was used:
1) For poultry sales,
2) For open-air sermons, presumably to keep the sermon deliverer dry in a downpour,
3) The most unlikely. As a washroom for priests. Rather draughty and not very private, I should have thought.

Whatever the reason, it certainly is a striking looking building.

The main reason for our journeys to Salisbury was to visit the cathedral and we were not disappointed. Before even entering the cathedral we spent a long time wandering round the outside and admiring the wonderful stonework. The west front, in particular, is very ornate with row upon row of statues in niches the whole height of the building. They were completed last century and replaced the originals. What an example of dedicated workmanship!

Although the spire on Norwich Cathedral seemed a great height the one on Salisbury Cathedral is the highest in England. I am always amazed at the intricate detail on very old buildings, especially cathedrals. Something I have often wondered is how it was possible to erect such a huge building in the fourteenth century. They certainly did not have the construction equipment we have today and yet the buildings are far superior in appearance to those of the present day and they have also stood the test of time.

The weather was very warm so we appreciated the cool, peaceful atmosphere within the cathedral. Some ancient churches and cathedrals are very dark but in Salisbury the huge columns of Purbeck stone in the high vaulted nave give it a wonderful light airy appearance.

There were several tombs and effigies and we were interested to discover that the oldest tomb is that of the Earl of Salisbury who was a witness at the signing of the Magna Carta in 1215. He brought a copy back to Salisbury and it is still held in the cathedral library. Another tomb is of a couple who were at the court of Elizabeth I. The husband was a courtier and his wife a maid of honour to the queen. It gave us a strange feeling to think these people lived all those centuries ago. We also thought much the same as we strolled along the cloisters and marvelled that people were walking in the same place seven hundred years ago.

In the two days of our visits to Salisbury we spent more time in the cathedral that in any other part of the city. It really is one of my favourite holiday memories.

Each year on our way south we had a short break at Stratford-on-Avon which gave us the opportunity to see the town and also leave the motorway and drive through the beautiful Cotswold countryside.

A mini disaster struck at the start of our first visit as I hurt my back when I bent down to pick up my suitcase. However, with my native doggedness taking control, I managed to hobble around, quite determined that mere backache was not going to spoil my first visit to the home of the Bard.

Most of the time, because of my disability, we drove around and did not stop off at the well-known places of interest. There was no urgency because we had promised ourselves to return there each year at the start of our annual journey to the south coast.

The lovely River Avon is one of the attractions of the town and we decided that a leisurely sail would be very pleasant, especially as the weather was quite hot and sticky. Because of my rigid state it was not an easy matter getting me into the craft but my husband and the boatman between them managed to lever me down. I was a few years off pension age but the amazing thing was, the senior citizens who joined us that day were hopping on and off the boat like five year olds while a crane would have been the best method for getting me on board.

I firmly believe that, because of the perversity of human nature, pupils who are asked to learn something will find any excuse to avoid studying and yet, left to their own devices, the opposite happens. This is particularly true as far as Shakespeare is concerned. I am quite sure that many people read the plays and appreciate the brilliance of his work far more after leaving school than they ever did when it was compulsory.

After our first unfortunate visit, spoiled by my small accident, we spent many happy times at Stratford.

Our time there was usually limited to two or three days which we enjoyed as we strolled around the town visiting the places of historical interest: Ann Hathaway's cottage, New Place where Shakespeare lived for several years before he died there, Mary Arden's house at Wilmcote, Trinity Church where he was baptized, and where he and several members of his family are buried, the Shakespeare Theatre and many more famous buildings.

We wondered, during our visit to Mary Arden's house, what that lady would have thought had she known her son's work would be part of the curriculum in schools throughout the world four hundred years later.

We were interested to see a dovecote beside the house and wondered if the present day occupiers are direct descendants of the original doves.

While staying in one hotel we were informed that *A Midsummer Night's Dream* was first performed in the grounds of what was then a manor house. However, we were later told that the first production was at a different location, so we felt the thing to do with such information was to take it 'with a pinch of salt'.

Stratford-on-Avon is such a lovely market town, with many beautiful half-timbered buildings, it would be well worth a visit even if Shakespeare had not been born and lived there.

One of the sixteenth century buildings we saw is Harvard House which has no Shakespeare connections as far as I know but is interesting nevertheless. Katherine Rogers, who lived there, married Robert Harvard and their son John emigrated to America and founded Harvard University. Many tourists from America visit the house each year.

The Cotswold countryside is very beautiful and that was the part of our journey south which we enjoyed most. After leaving Stratford we had our first stop at Moreton-on-Marsh with its Mitford connections. The Resesdale Hall is in the centre of the small town. On our last visit there we had morning tea in the White Hart Hotel where Charles I slept in 1643. I wonder if he really slept in all the places where he is supposed to have done. Perhaps it is like Mary Queen of Scots in Scotland where some of the castles and stately homes containing her bed were not even built until after her death. Maybe I am being too cynical to suggest such a thing.

During one of our visits to Moreton-on-Marsh we stood in the crowd by the roadside as a pipe band made its way along the main street. My husband said, 'why the tears? It's not even a Scottish band.' My reply was, 'they're playing, (sob sob), "The Scottish Soldier", (sob sob), and I'm just so proud.' Now, I am not a weepy sort of person, in fact during times of stress I am usually very calm. However, all my life I have been deeply moved when the bagpipes were played, especially when the pipe band was marching along. Cynics reading this will probably say it is the noise which brings the tears. They would be wrong as it is sheer Scottish, or more accurately, Highland pride at the sight of kilted bandsmen playing such stirring music.

One year, on our way from Sandbanks, we stopped at a small café in Melksham for a cup of tea. We waited some time for the bill so eventually my husband said to the waitress, 'I wonder if I could settle the bill now as we are going to Scotland and we are anxious to be on our way.' I think the young girl was of the opinion that Scotland was a wild hostile country because she shook my husband's hand and wished him 'Good Luck'. We felt she must have believed cattle rustling and freebooting were still rife in Scotland.

CHAPTER 10

I have mentioned our holiday in Shetland but there are two other Scottish islands, namely Skye and Iona, whose names bring back very happy memories of times spent on both.

The first time I visited Skye was with an aunt who had recently been widowed. She and her husband had spent many camping holidays on Skye and she wanted to make a sentimental journey to the island.

I mentioned earlier about my aversion to travel by small boat but driving on to a ferry is another one of my pet hates. As we waited on the pier at Kyle of Lochalsh there was a large cattle truck slowly driven on to the ferry boat. I took it for granted that the other truck sitting alongside would then be waved on and we, along with the other cars, would have to wait for the next boat.

The butterflies in my stomach, therefore, worked overtime when I heard the man who was guiding the traffic shout, 'the Mini next.' It was worse than my driving test as I edged my way on to the ferry, knowing that there was a queue of people watching the operation with interest. As far as I was concerned matters got worse as the next truck arrived on my other side. This meant I was sandwiched between the two great trucks, like a small biscuit between two large slices of bread.

My passenger, on the other hand, seemed quite unconcerned but, being a non-driver, it may have been a case of 'where ignorance is bliss, etc'. Of course, after spending many holidays living in a tiny white tent and enduring days of wind and rain on Skye, this would have been a tame experience.

However, after the ferry incident, our holiday turned out to be really enjoyable. Nearly every corner of Skye has legends or stories of historical interest connected with it and many of those stories have something to do with the Clan Donald.

As my aunt was my father's sister we were both members of the Clan Donald and so had especial interest in the island.

Skye is known as the Misty Isle, or in the Gaelic, *Eilean a' Cheo* (Island of Mist); it is very aptly named. I have known many rainy days, but when the sun shines the whole island seems to light up and everywhere appears to be sparkling clean. I think most islands are worth a visit but, to me, Skye is special and, without doubt, my favourite.

Skye must have more places of historical interest per acre than anywhere else in Britain. I know that my aunt and I had a special interest because of our Clan Donald connection but, during our holiday we met tourists from all over the world, some of whom had already visited the Highlands, and especially Skye, several times.

We stayed in Portree which got its name when King James visited Skye in the sixteenth century. It was originally called by the Gaelic name Port-an-Righ (Port of the King) which was later changed to Portree.

We found this a good central point from where we travelled each day to visit places of interest. A month would not be enough so during our week's sojourn our daily journeys had to be carefully planned beforehand.

We decided on two of especial interest - Kilmuir in the north and Dunvegan on the west side of the island.

In Kilmuir is the Skye Museum of Island Life comprising several thatched cottages built and furnished as exact replicas of houses lived in by crofters and their families.

There is the main croft house, a weaver's house, a barn, and of special interest to us, a smithy, or smiddy where the blacksmith plied his trade and kept his customers and any passers-by up to date with all the local news and gossip. I understand the smiddy was a meeting-place for local people all over the Highlands and, the smith himself, when horses were used by rich and poor alike, was a very busy man. However, he could always stop for a few minutes to have a break and chat to his customers.

When we left the cottages it was like entering another world – having stepped back in time during the previous hour and living a crofter's life of more than a century ago.

After leaving the Museum of Island Life we walked to Kilmuir cemetery which is a short distance away. Our main reason for this was to visit the grave of Flora MacDonald and her husband Allan. Most people know the story of Flora MacDonald and Bonnie Prince Charlie after the Battle of Culloden but I suspect they, like me, knew little more apart from the fact that she went to America.

As I said before, history is much more interesting when stories are related by local people who have re-told them many times. We certainly found this to be true on our first visit to Skye.

Some time after Prince Charlie was safely in France Flora was captured and questioned about her involvement with the prince. She made a full confession and was eventually held in the Tower of London for several months. After her release she spent some time in Edinburgh before her return to Skye where she married Allan MacDonald of Kingsburgh.

Many years after the Jacobite Rebellion Flora and Allan left Skye to start a new life in America. By that time they had a large family of seven children. Two of their sons accompanied them and it was arranged that relatives would care for the remaining members of their family.

They stayed there for only a few years because the American War of Independence started and Allan joined the Loyalist army. He was taken prisoner but eventually was released and allowed to leave the country. They sailed for Britain and finally settled once more in Skye. Sadly, their time there was short as Flora died in 1790 and Allan followed two years later.

On my last visit to Skye I stayed in the Royal Hotel, Portree. I discovered that in the eighteenth century the hotel was called MacNab's Inn and it was there that Flora said farewell to the prince in July 1746.

Our other main outing was to Dunvegan Castle, home of the Chiefs of Clan MacLeod. The chief at the time we visited was Dame Flora MacLeod of MacLeod, a most remarkable lady. She travelled the world, visiting members of her clan and telling people about Skye and particularly Dunvegan Castle. She certainly must have helped the Scottish tourist industry.

There are many tales about the history of Dunvegan, some quite gory, and many of those about violent feuds between members of the

Clan MacLeod and their great rivals, Clan Donald..

One story I think is better known than any of the others and a happy tale rather than a tragic one. Legend has it a chief in the fourteenth century had a fairy wife and they lived in Fairyland. After some time had passed the chief decided he wanted to return to the human world.

When she was saying a tearful goodbye the fairy wife gave her husband a banner which, she told him, could be waved three times if he was in danger and its magic powers would save him or any other MacLeod Chief. To date the flag has been used twice in this way so it can be put in practice one more time.

I read about the MacLeods of Dunvegan many years before my first visit to Skye and so was familiar with the legend of the Fairy Flag. However, I never imagined it to be the tattered remnant of silk which we were shown in its case. I should have known that something which was six hundred years old could not be in pristine condition despite having magic powers.

I returned to Skye several times and on each occasion I discovered that, for me, the magic of the island was as strong as ever. On my last visit, as I mentioned earlier, I again stayed in Portree. It was, of necessity, a solitary trip, made for sentimental reasons, when I travelled by bus from Inverness to Portree.

One day during my stay I joined an organized coach tour from Portree to Kilmuir. I was really re-tracing my steps but this time travelled by coach rather than private car as I had done previously. The driver, an Englishman who had lived on Skye for several years, also acted as courier and was an excellent guide — describing places of historical interest as we travelled through the countryside.

I believe I was the only Scot on the tour and many of the passengers had travelled from the Far East to see Scotland and especially the Misty Isle. I think the fact that it really was a misty isle that day added the true feeling of drama to the stories the driver had to tell.

The rain teemed down all day but it stopped shortly before we returned to Portree and when we finally arrived there was a beautiful rainbow as if framing the bay. A wonderful ending to an interesting day, especially for our foreign friends. I am by no means an expert with the camera but, as my bedroom overlooked the bay I took a photograph to remind me that grey days do come to an end.

I visited the island of Iona on three occasions and each time I travelled by a different route. My first visit was over thirty years ago and I also had my first camping experience at that time.

My sister, her husband and three children were spending a holiday with us in Inverness and invited me to go camping with them. I had never stayed in a tent before then so thought it might be a good idea.

We intended spending the first night on a campsite near Oban and then have a few days on Mull from where we could cross to Iona.

It was sunny when we left home but the rain started by the time we reached Fort William. As we were all optimists we were pretty certain it would clear up so we continued on our way. The rain, however, had other ideas and continued to pour. It was a miracle that my brother-in-law managed to erect the couple of tents as, to quote the TV weathermen, the weather was atrocious. Despite the wind and rain we did eventually settle down in our sleeping bags and sheer exhaustion made us have a few hours sleep.

Our main aim was to visit Iona and, in spite of the bad weather, we decided to go ahead with our planned expedition. We left the car at Oban and caught the steamer to Mull. We eventually arrived at Fionnphort where we met a local man who took us by rowing boat to Iona. As I mentioned before, I am not a lover of small boats but the crossing was short and the sea calm so we had quite a pleasant trip.

The rain had stopped by then and the sun was shining so my first impression of Iona was of a beautiful island. It was as though the whole world was lit up and I think was emphasized because it was a complete contrast to the previous day. The sun making the water sparkle, the white sands and the amazing sense of peace as we stepped ashore still remains one of my happiest memories.

As our outdoor clothing was still soaking wet we decided it would not be sensible to have another night under canvas. Anyway, the tents had no chance to dry off so, after our visit to Iona, we made our way back to Inverness.

My next trip to Iona was an organized tour which started by coach from Inverness to Fort William. We then had a very pleasant sail down the west coast to Oban, picked up more passengers and on to Mull where a small boat took us from Fionnphort across to Iona. What a pleasant sound Fionnphort has - exactly right for that lovely part of the country!

The third time my husband and I were spending a few days at Oban when we decided to visit Iona. As we waited on the pier for the steamer to arrive we watched a seal in the harbour, not at all shy of all the bustle and noise as traffic passed along and people chatted as they stood around. The seal appeared to be taking an interest in all the goings on as it bobbed up and down in the water, almost as though that was its daily routine.

The sense of peace returned each time I visited Iona and I feel the thousands of visitors to the island each year from all parts of the world probably get the same impression.

When Saint Columba and his twelve followers arrived in 563 it was certainly peaceful and had been for a long time, for the Druids used to worship there. However, a couple of hundred years after Columba's arrival the Vikings, during several raids, plundered and destroyed the Abbey buildings and on one occasion murdered over sixty monks at what is now called Martyr's Bay.

It is impossible to understand why men behave in such a barbaric way yet today, over a thousand years later, the same thing is happening in many parts of the world. I find it very strange that Saint Columba brought Christianity and, I suppose, civilization to Scotland and now his own native land is one of those places where such horrendous and murderous crimes are frequently committed.

There are many legends of Saint Columba's visit to Inverness when he converted King Brude to Christianity. Many are believable but there are some, when certain miracles were performed, which could only be accepted with the proverbial pinch of salt.

One story in particular is often re-told, especially in summer when the latest sighting of Nessie coincides with the arrival of the first tourists. Although that remark may sound cynical I firmly believe there is a large animal in Loch Ness and it may well be that it hibernates in winter.

To return to the story of Columba, a monster lived in the River Ness and Columba saw one of its victims being buried by the riverside. I assume it was a vegetarian and just killed for fun. Columba was determined to cure the monster of its evil ways so he ordered one of his followers to swim across the river and collect a boat on the other side. The purpose of this request is not clear.

The monster, which seems to have been similar to a shark with huge jaws (probably like in the well-known film) went towards Saint Columba's man with its jaws open ready to pounce. Saint Columba then made the sign of the cross and the creature fled.

I attended a memorial service recently in a church near Aviemore where there is a bell reputed to have belonged to Saint Columba. It certainly looks very old, is black iron and slightly broken. It is not the same shape as present day bells but rather like the cowbells seen on the continent.

CHAPTER 11

As we lived in an industrial town we sometimes felt the need to get away at week-ends. One of our favourite haunts was Pitlochry and we took advantage of the week-end bargain breaks offered by the same firm doing the London ones which I mentioned previously.

The main purpose of our visit was to see the current plays in the Pitlochry Theatre, which must be in one of the loveliest settings of any theatre in Britain. Each year we were sent the programme for the whole season so we found it very exciting to choose the plays we wished to see and also the dates. I always wrote a note to enclose with the cheque and within a week usually received the tickets.

On our way to Pitlochry we added a touch of luxury to the week-end by calling at Gleneagles Hotel for morning tea. I think we always expected to spot a celebrity but I'm afraid in that respect our hopes were dashed.

I was normally very careful regarding theatre tickets but on one occasion I think the excitement of the week-end or the proposed visit to Gleneagles made me forgetful. While having tea, a frantic search in my handbag revealed the fact that I had left the tickets at home. As we had by then gone more than half-way we decided to continue to Pitlochry.

We called at the theatre before going to our hotel and explained the situation to the girl at the box office and I must say, for sheer brilliance and efficiency she deserved a medal. We quite expected to pay for seats over again if there were any available.

The girl asked if I sent a letter when requesting the tickets and when I answered in the affirmative she checked the letters which she held and was able to give us duplicate tickets as she had noted seat numbers on my letter. I may not have been the only theatre-goer with a lapse of memory so probably precautions were always taken. We were certainly very impressed with the service and were able to enjoy our dinner at the hotel before seeing an excellent performance at the theatre.

Each spring we rented a cottage in Nethybridge for a week. It had woodland behind and a heather moor in front with views of the Cairngorms in the background. We loved our holidays there and were like two rather ancient babes in the wood. We enjoyed the peace and were not at all bothered by the isolation.

Our neighbours were the deer who lived in the wood beside the cottage. They were quite bold and each morning they stood outside the kitchen window, having jumped over the fence. We wondered if previous inhabitants of the cottage had fed them as the deer appeared regularly each morning. Perhaps they felt it was their domain and we were interlopers.

The cottage was lovely and had been modernized and we considered ourselves very lucky to have found it. A friend did an oil painting of it from a photograph and it still hangs in my living-room and is a constant reminder of happy days.

It was a central point for us to tour the area and also to visit members of my family. Grantown-on-Spey, Carrbridge, Aviemore were within easy reach and Inverness was not too far away.

As we did self-catering I once more adopted the girl guide motto and was well prepared, packing everything except the kitchen sink. There were boxes of food, bedlinen, personal clothing in cases, and one year a portable TV set. The reason for the last item was, we enjoyed watching certain programmes although we could never be called addicts. Imagine our surprise when we discovered a TV had been installed since our last visit! We had a small car and, because of the TV set, space was even more limited than usual. A friend lent us a roof rack, something we had never used before that time.

That year we decided to return home by a different route instead of the A9. We joined the A939 which passed close to the cottage and went by Tomintoul (well known for radio and TV weather reports in winter) then took a side road which brought us out at Crathie Church, where the Royal Family worship. We visited the church and afterwards walked to Balmoral Castle which is close by. We then had a lovely run by Deeside where we had a picnic by the river. It was a beautiful day and, we thought, a perfect ending to our holiday but fate decreed otherwise.

We finally joined the A9 and stopped in Auchterarder for food supplies. When I returned to the car with my purchases my husband said, 'bad news, we've lost a case off the roof rack and guess which one?' I knew it must be mine as it was on top and I also remembered with horror the way I threw all the dirty washing into it. I had a mental picture of it lying open by the roadside and all the people in cars seeing the pathetic contents.

We met a policeman in the main street. I think doing his first walkie-talkie job. He called Perth police station and was told the case had been handed in by a motorist. We were by then sixteen miles south of Perth so altogether thirty-two miles were added to our journey.

I hadn't locked the case as, naturally, I hadn't anticipated losing it so the police were able to check the items inside, much to my embarrassment. If it had happened on our outward journey all would have been well as the garments were at that time clean, ironed and neatly folded. On the return they were soiled, crumpled and thrown in anyhow. I suppose it was just another case of airing one's dirty linen in public.

There was something good to compensate for the disaster. As we were going to be home much later than expected we called at a fish and chip shop on our return to Auchterarder and bought chicken and chips. I am not a chip person but I must say, sitting in a lay-by, eating our chicken suppers, was an enjoyable and memorable experience.

Some women are born housewives, taking great pride in all aspects of housekeeping and their homes are a delight to visit. I regret to say I would never win an Oscar for domesticity although I do like a clean house. Every so often while we were working my aversion to housework surfaced and I suppose at those times I could be called 'The Great Moaner' or 'Moanalot', like a well-known character in an old radio programme.

After a tiring day at the office I would attempt to produce an appetizing meal which never quite turned out the same as those in the beautiful pictures shown in the various cookery books. I had a drawerful of those, being ever the optimist and quite certain that one day my culinary effort would be as good as, if not better than, the experts.

I remember a friend saying after I described one more calamity in the kitchen, 'but you're good at sweets.' The trouble was, a delicious pudding could never compensate for a disastrous main course, when what was supposedly a tender lamb turned out to be an old sheep.

I exaggerate, of course, as the majority of our meals were reasonable but like most cooks, disaster did strike from time to time. I would then say something like, 'I wish I was anywhere but here,' and my husband, ever the diplomat, countered that remark with, 'never mind, I'll take you home gain, Kathleen', and as Catherine is my middle name the song was quite appropriate.

In 1987 he was as good as his word because we really did return to my homeland and the wheel had by then turned full circle. I was born in the Highlands and after many years wandering here and there, I returned to my favourite place on earth.

Some people can search for years but we were lucky to find our ideal retirement home in a very short time. It is situated in what must be one of the loveliest villages in Britain, with glorious views of the Moray Firth and the Ross-shire hills in the background. I once more look across to Ben Wyvis from home.

Our house was without a name so, after giving much thought to the subject, we decided to call it, Innisfree. We both liked the poem by W.B. Yeats and especially the line, 'And I shall have some peace there, for peace comes dropping slow'. It seemed very apt because we found a place which is secluded but not isolated and was like heaven after living in a bustling industrial town.

We often said that we would like a dog and we achieved that ambition, too. We acquired a black labrador puppy and as the house has an Irish name we decided to call him 'Paddy'. He would never make a guard dog as he gives a great welcome to friend and stranger alike but he is quite a character and a faithful companion.

We settled in our new home and loved the simple lifestyle, especially as it was a complete contrast to our previous one.

We were new to gardening but enjoyed it and had a great deal of help from books borrowed from the local library and tips given by TV and radio garden experts. In this way we were able to produce some vegetables and have a decent show of flowers.

There are lovely walks in the woods behind the house and also on Culloden Battlefield which is a short distance away. The main reason for our walks was Paddy, who needed daily exercise but we, also, enjoyed the outings.

We drove out to local beauty spots and other places of interest and in this area there are plenty of those. I was happy to introduce my husband to places which were familiar to me but new to him.

EPILOGUE

We had four idyllic years but then my husband became ill. He did not suffer long. He died as he had lived, with quiet dignity and in the loving care of the nursing staff of the Highland Hospice. He would have had expert medical care in any hospital but the love given by the dedicated hospice staff makes each patient feel extra special.

The Highland Hospice is more like a home than a hospital and it is there because of the generosity of the Highland people.

I was quite devastated at the time and can understand why people in similar circumstances resort to alcohol or drugs to shut out reality. However, with the wonderful support of both my own and my husband's family I managed to survive such a traumatic time. I also have good friends and kind neighbours who all offered to give me any assistance I required.

Paddy and I are now on our own and we still have our daily walks. He loves the car and sits proudly in the back seat during my shopping expeditions and when I visit family and friends. As I said earlier, he is a faithful companion.

I knew that self-pity would not help me and would be boring for other people. I then decided to start writing as much as I knew about the early part of our family history. It continued from there and it has taken me a couple of years to complete.

I found it of great therapeutic value and it has helped to remind me of so many happy times. As I look back on the written pages I realize that, apart from the last few years, I've been lucky to have had a good and interesting life.

As someone once said, 'Memories give one a second chance of happiness.'